The Mare and the Mouse

The Mare and the Mouse

*S*tories of My Horses: Volume I

Written and Illustrated by
Martín Prechtel

 North Star Press of St. Cloud

Library of Congress CIP data available upon request.

First Edition
ISBN: 978-1-68201-117-1

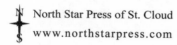 North Star Press of St. Cloud
www.northstarpress.com

Printed in the United States of America.

Cover painting: *Mother of Horses Bringing Home the Infant Sun and Moon*, by Martín Prechtel.
All text and interior line drawings by Martín Prechtel.
Japanese calligraphy by Reed Larsen.
Cover design and interior layout by Liz Dwyer of North Star Press.

Type set in Times New Roman, headings set in Brioso, and Brioso Semibold Italic.

Library of Congress Control Number: 2021931042

Table of Contents

Notice

All three volumes of the *Stories of My Horses* are meant as an overdue love letter and tribute to all the horses of my life and my beloved New Mexico for the spiritual nourishment and down-to-earth vitality that like a beautiful warm blanket has kept me warm and hopeful through the cold cynical blizzard of modernity's compromised sense of wonder.

While every adventure, misadventure, and episode found in these books took place precisely where and how they are described, I have taken the liberty of assigning alternative names for most but not all of the humans in my eternal faith that even mean people can change for the better, but also to protect the sweeter kind from any retribution from those that won't change and to respect the privacy of the shy. None of the horse's names have been changed so they can be remembered again by those who knew them.

Disclaimer

Neither the Publisher nor the Author accepts any liability for any mishaps, accidents, or any damages to people, property, or animals occurring from anyone who after reading the *Stories of My Horses* is erroneously led to act on any of the opinions expressed herein as advice of any type or who foolishly decides that they should try to re-enact any of the episodes described in these books in their own lives!

While We Were Riding, We Were Singing

A Horse Song:

(everyone sing)

For the never-ending wild land.
For the never-ending wild land.
For the never-ending wild land.
For the never-ending wild land.

For the wide-open ride.
For the wide-open ride.
For the wide-open ride.
For the wide-open ride.

For our horses' never-ending wild epic hearts, ridden by a
truly wide-open mind.
For our horses' never-ending wild epic hearts, ridden by a
truly wide-open mind.
For our horses' never-ending wild epic hearts, ridden by a
truly wide-open mind.
For our horses' never-ending wild epic hearts, ridden by a
truly wide-open mind.

Into every hoof print that we leave, may seeds of rich spiritual
substance fall.
Into every hoof print that we leave, may seeds of rich spiritual
substance fall.

Into every hoof print that we leave, may seeds of rich spiritual
substance fall.
Into every hoof print that we leave, may seeds of rich spiritual
substance fall.

To sprout a time of hope beyond our own.
To sprout a time of hope beyond our own.
To sprout a time of hope beyond our own.
To sprout a time of hope beyond our own.

Let the world jump back to life.
Let the world jump back to life.
Let the world jump back to life.
Let the world jump back to life.

(Please repeat — singing)

A Dedication

Because the undeniable presence of Pueblo people's early expertise with the old magnificent breed of horse on which their European oppressors arrived has been consciously and unfairly diminished, dismissed, or completely written out of the record of horse history by Euro-American academics, all three books of this series *Stories of My Horses*, are dedicated to the Tewa, Tiwa, Towa, Ashiwi, and especially the Keres speaking villages of the area now called New Mexico. These Pueblo people were indisputably the very first North American First Nation tribes to ever ride, drive, own, and raise horses. Despite four and a half centuries of colonial oppression, it was the original Native Pueblo people's continued proficiency with, reverence for, and adoption of the old Spanish *Mesta*-raised horses into the heart of their spiritual lives that actually converted these unique horses right out from under their own would-be religious converters, turning the colonialist's animals into the very different and fine Native horses they became. Either directly or indirectly it was from these Pueblo herds that *all* the great Native horse cultures—of the Plains, Prairies, and Northwest, of the entire American and Canadian west—received their first "indigified horses" upon whose backs their renowned mobility sky rocketed into the prominence their memory still maintains in the history of the North American Native West.

Chapter 1

Knowing the Way Home

Though horses are beautiful and it doesn't take much to see why so many people love horses as much as they do, there is a deeper and grief-ridden reason for the strong obsession people have for horses.

Maybe some of this has to do with how much power and potential for freedom resides in every horse. Horses just breathe ions of freedom into us stirring some strong ancestral memory of our mutual history when anciently we ranged together as free beings, when only the grass, the wind, the wolves, and swans called the shots, where the air was clean, the stream water drinkable, the land fat with wild animals. Stored in some special forgotten chamber of our hearts we must have the old memory of how horses saved our own ancestors from the generations of captive slavery and stationary servitude at the hands of settled empires. Horses gave them the liberty of tribal mobility and a nobility on the unfarmed, uncitified Eurasian steppe, where with only the Holy sky as their container, away from the chains, whips, and plows, somewhere inside us, we know that horses saved us. At least for a millennia.

And all of that is true.

But along with all of that there is something else that all horse people know. Something even more significant than liberty that the presence of horses keeps alive in that part of us that is capable of hope.

This is the fact that no matter how far they are forced to flee, all horses can always find their way home.

Horses always run, meander, or pick their way home. They know the way home too; they don't have to guess. No matter how many landmarks have changed, gone missing, covered in snow, no matter how many new obstacles there may be, horses, like migrating birds and butterflies, have the direction home written in their beings.

For a wild horse, of course, home is not only a place, but in the herd, in that place. Separated by many, many miles such a horse can always eventually find "his herd". And the collective mind of a displaced wild horse herd can always find its way back to its own water, its land, its personal preferred atmosphere. Horses love being at home on the earth. And they love being at home together.

Often a person becomes the horse's herd, then wherever you are is where his horse's herd is living. Separated from you and given an opportunity and unhindered, your horse will generally show up back at your place.

You are the herd.

If you are very close to your animals and for some reason you disappear from the "herd home" without first explaining to them that you're going on book tour for three weeks and you'll be back soon, they may get worried and without a word to your ranch's intern break out of their confines and go looking for you, coursing like a cloud of swallows in the very direction they last saw you heading, trying to catch up to you, because since you're their herd, wherever you are is home for them! This has happened many times with my own horses.

But as humans we have changed and find ourselves fettered by fear and spirit loss in the mythologically disconnected existence that settled civilization has forced modern people to bear. We ourselves have been lost for a long strange time: lost from our real selves, lost from the spiritual intact people we have always been meant to be, lost from such people's ability to be at home, becoming instead cultures of restless war and acquisition-addicted people, inventing technology to flee from our ability to be tribally in love with being at home, losing our pre-citified existence at the speed of civilization's toxic sprawl in search of a technological Shangri-La or some heaven in a future that we can never catch up to. For that reason I don't think we people really love horses so much for their promise of freedom to get us away from what we fear, as much as we love horses because deep down some part of us knows that though horses have come the journey with us, unlike us, they still remember what we have forgotten and so desperately need, for once you're on a horse, no matter how far you may have wandered from your real self, your horse always knows the way Home.

Chapter 2

Fire and Horses

Of all the domesticated animals of the millennia past with whom people have associated and depended on, horses continue to hold a mental prominence in the consciousness of many cultures that differs from those of dogs, cats, cows, goats, ducks, turkeys, chickens, pigs, or sheep. Even in the psyches of people of modern cities and suburbs, where flesh and blood horses are completely absent or present only in the most limited and affectated fashion, horses still strangely inspire firmly held opinions about what horses really are. Derived mostly from the commonly held prejudices of their ancestors from by-gone-days, these opinions are preserved in the family myths as fact, though these suburbanites may have absolutely no idea what real-life horses are like.

Even horse people who do ride and own or work horses everyday are not immune to vehemently defending the most unreliable notions about the history of "their own particular breed" and can be very tribalist and aggressively biased about the so-called "deficiencies" and lesser history of "other breeds". Otherwise sane-seeming individuals, when it comes to horses, will fiercely defend the most worn-out dogmatic propaganda as "the only truth" against a million other experts with diverse opposing opinions "backed up by science". Most horse people would probably agree on only one thing and that is that they are right!

This is not only because people are by nature irrational but because horses are dear to us and ancient with us in a way different and more magical than some animals. Their presence lives on in the memory of our ancestral souls, not so much in our conscious minds. When our "opinions" start using today's science to defend their personal prejudices, we are on troubled ground. Our souls on the other hand don't serve imperial prejudices; they know the histories because they are our history. Our souls have anciently lived out what our minds have an opinion about. Our souls don't care about the "truth" of our opinions. They want a mythological link-up with an everyday immersion into the magic of the natural, unpeopled wild that our ancestral Indigenous origins lived in forever. And in the wild landscape of our pasts, our souls still ride their horses of memory. Because of this, horses have a lot in common with wild land, with wind, water, and most of all, with our ancient tribal fire. For all of these live inside us, *not* as things or metaphors of psychological functions, but as mythic heroes riding mythic horses around the mythic campground of our mythic souls.

Horses have been with us when we were all nomads gathered nightly at our people's fires. Not like cars or motorcycles parked inanimately around our fires, but as living allies and companions upon whose backs living our lives depended. As our tribal companions, horses have learned from people to cherish our campfires. When all their ancient equine instinct says FLEE, to flee the smoke and the night flame, a horse that has daily carried you far from home will never flee your company at the night's cooking fire, but always stays nearby, comforted by the fire and the murmur of your voice telling extravagant tales by the fireside.

It is very old, this friendship we people and our horses have with story and fire camped together throughout our history. A campfire that still lives inside the landscape of the souls of many of us.

More than anything else, I know that both horses and fire generate in humankind an unavoidable manic need in our thalamus, pituitary, thyroid and adrenal hormones to both tell and hear fabulously ornate stories and to outdo one another in an endless stream of stories.

Build a fire anywhere. Build it in the dark. Make it a small one. Boil water. Maybe make tea or coffee, cook something. What happens?

People start showing up. They ask you what the fire's for; you hand them tea and you start explaining. A story has already begun. Maybe even the fire marshal shows up, you start explaining, then he starts explaining about what could happen and what did happen over there and off we go. Pretty soon everybody is there; stories are circulating. Fires and stories and warm liquids.

Now do the same thing with horses. Bring over a horse, then ask anybody who rides or raises horses, I mean *any* question about her or his horse, and away we go. It won't really even matter if the person's young or old because the stories will never end.

God forbid if you ever have the audacity to build a fire, cook some food, make coffee or tea and invite even just five people who love horses and five who know nothing about horses and tie your old mare to a tree thirty feet away. Once the stories start up, all ten of these people will be experts about riding and adventures on animals they've never seen, ridden, fed, or even previously thought about. Within twenty minutes, everyone will be clamoring to outdo each other. Behaving just like the horses themselves who love to outrun each other, coursing off crazy in any direction in the wind, the people at a horse-story-fire will run off at the mouth in love with running stories together, claiming experiences and stories about which they know absolutely nothing. Like horses, they are happy and full of life.

Its not just because horses and fire inspire us together to make delicious, competitive, absurd B.S. It's because horses and fire are housed in our souls inseparably and together. Horses and our souls are heroic: they want to run, jump, and be admired. To us, all horses are real mythological beings, unconsciously in our memory from a time when humans were still intact and psychologically more sturdy beings in love with beauty: humans in a world not yet run and ruined by urbanity. That part of us that has been cloaked by modernity's blasé, everyday, synthetic unnaturalness can't block the stories that fire, horses, and hot tea cause to bubble up in us past modernity's rationalist roadblock. For these stories are the soul's campaign to resurrect the young hero in us, or the old champion in us, or the Mother of Horses on the endless-uncultivated-grassy steppe to fly again with the liquid whinny of a deeper indigenous being, to somehow thrive again as a real person, beyond the cardboard cut-out personality the world has tried to pound us into.

Horses force us to become consciously mythological, to ride hard, stand around looking good, rest proud, and to be friendly and intact again at the fire, even when we are absolutely ignorant how sweet a live horse smells like, much less feels like dangerously coursing light-speed under the moon!

Well... this book is nothing more than a small campfire around whose flames the horses that kept me vital come back into view again, one story at a time, one after the next, each one adding to the last, until like a fire themselves around whose tales we drink more and more of life's crazy tea, in whose brew, all my horses dead and alive yet run as a single herd upon whose epic backs I share the ride with all those who have ridden and rested at my fire and those who never have and wishing they might, can somehow do just by listening.

Because times are bad for what is magical in Nature and people, someone has got to build the first campfire, sing the first epic tune, and start up the stories that tell such a world back into life all over again.

So please come sit by my fire,

Have some tea,

And

Like my great-grandmother Louisa said:

"Boy, never let the dry truth get in the way of the telling of the story of what actually happened."

So...

This is what happened...

Chapter 3
Louisa

My mother was an educator her entire short life. First and foremost, a teacher by love and predilection, then as a creator of Native American language programs, after which a principal, then a school superintendent, my short, willful, beautiful, strategizing dark-haired mother identified entirely with her multination Indian blood courageously creating and locating funding to instigate and dig up forgotten laws to enforce programs for Native American education in public schools that included not destroying Native culture when such a thing was totally a back burner consideration.

In a way, I guess, she was following a tradition of inspired female liberty and determination which, as it usually does in a family, jumped a generation from her grandmother to my mother.

Though she would later become very learned and educated "white man style", the summers of my mother's early days as a kid were spent with her grandmother Louisa on her ranch. The mother of her father, she gave her that "other" education everybody needs: a learning on the ground, in the ground, on the land, learning in and among her grandmother's plants and animals, immersing her into many spoken languages, both Native and European, and above all, an older magical tradition with horses that was wound up inextricably with that beautiful old woman's obsession with the history of everything!

My great-grandmother's personal adaptation of her Native legacy, in which tribal women had always been in charge of the corn fields, animals, houses, children, horses, and the tribal remembrances of all those things, had the addition of her grand sense of self-worth and unsinkable conviction that people had an obligation to not only be in love with being alive with all your beasts and plants, but in love with the story of where it all comes from, Native or not. These, I think, were the major mantras and seeds of hope to which my mother desperately clutched throughout her otherwise loveless younger days that kept the little steamboat of her soul spiritually stoked to paddle through the sad muck of many imagination-squashing years.

My great-grandmother was tough, they say, fierce to the cruel, grand to the grand, sweet to the innocent. But in a way mysterious to all, with her ever present corn cob tobacco pipe

of her own manufacture still clenched in her ancient determined teeth till the minute she died, close to a hundred, she
was something elegant and beguiling in her own aristocratic
definition of what being a beautiful woman actually meant.

She owned a ranching farm of Indian corn, tobacco, a
great bunch of cattle, chickens, and a stable of horses. Up
in the early-morning dark, tackling all the hands-on work
that such an endeavor entails, she was nonetheless always
back into her voluminous silk gowns, lace caps, gloves, and
boundless supply of her beloved cut, red garnets that she wore
everyday, by the pound, head to foot, all in time to boil the
kettle for mid-morning tea, which she never missed. (People often forget how much tea many American Natives still
continue to drink, especially those whose ancestors had allied
with the British early on). This tireless, classy, garnet-stud-
ded, silk-wearing matron, having already worn-out and buried three husbands, was above all else, a woman of horses.
A woman who rode and drove horses, a woman who broke
horses, a woman who thought horses were just another word
for history.

It was old Louisa herself who taught my young mother to sit straight in the saddle and carry herself like a lady
general. She taught her to love horses, to love riding across
the wild unfenced land teaching her that by riding well you
could outstrip Hell, outrun mediocrity, and become your own
person. She was taught that if she did it right, the horse and
her, just standing proud and excellent, would by sheer force
of nature and beauty melt away the limiting command of what

society insisted she become and turn her into the force she was really meant to be.

While my mother learned mostly to ride astride with leather pants, quirt, and tall boots, Louisa also taught her to ride in silk gowns, with fancy shoes, and a pinned-on hat all fluffed and flounced, upon a 19th century, white-lady's side-saddle, crop in hand, just to round out her education, while checking for downed fences on the ranch! While they rode everyday all summer together they also milked cows, gathered eggs, and butchered chickens. They rode only Louisa's own breed of horses. Horses born, bred, raised, and trained on the ancestral land, from ancestrally handed-down horses, where my mother's father had been born, but where now only the old woman lived and thrived. It was this ancestral land which became synonymous with the family's old, garnet-wearing, ancestral mother, where my own mother had spent fifteen flamboyant, beautiful summers riding and absorbing the oral and written histories of every known thing according to Louisa, away from the bleak, unencouraging, down-in-the-mouth, cookie-cutter, mid-western, repressive life her parents tried to lead in Detroit.

Louisa taught my mother that people were born precious, but they were not born as people. One had to be cooked by life and do a lot of things to qualify as a person.

In our case, my brother and I, until we could ride well, we were not considered truly people yet, we weren't completed, we were still "unfinished children". This must have been great-grandma Louisa's idea of "finishing school". So our mother taught us both to ride and not to forget that: "A man on foot is no man at all, unless of course his horse's name is Foot."

Chapter 4

The Horse as Water Monster

New Mexico was my world when I was young and that world was big, but all the people were short and their places sparsely dotted the lands along the few rivers of our world, especially the Rio Grande. Otherwise, the great cobbly hills, tall fir-covered snowy mountains, mystic sandstone cliffs, volcanic plugs, and lava fields went on forever, wide open.

You could walk or ride for days if you wanted and never run into another human, unless of course you wanted to. And if you did, most likely you already knew them. There were so few people in the whole state then that everybody knew everybody or they knew someone who did.

Along that Rio Grande the Indian officials of the tribe on whose land I grew up on allowed our family to live in the compound of the school some five miles from their village where my mother taught the "special" class. They only allowed outsiders, other Natives, or non-tribal members to visit by day, but not to live on their reservation. We were a fortunate exception. As a kid I wandered that wild open land interminably, giving my parents a lot of worries. I'd often disappear overnight alone or appear with friends at some other Pueblo's ceremonial dance twenty miles away.

Farmers first and foremost, silversmiths, and creators of shell and turquoise bead necklaces by fame, and cattle raisers in a more minimal way, the Pueblo was a vibrant, off-limits, secret, ritual town of great complexity and spiritual wealth.

But when it came time to plow and plant their fields of chile, for which they were also justly famous, since nobody at that time owned a tractor or any of the implements, many families would communally hire one with a driver from a neighboring Spanish village.

But even with the appearance of a tribal tractor in the 1950's and 60's, there were people who preferred to create the furrows for their combined corn, melon, chile, and squash fields by means of an old moldboard plow pulled by a single, famous, white horse of at least sixteen hands or more.

Now, all the herd horses on the east side of the Big River were little Spanish horses, clearly the old Barb, the so-called Indian-Ponies people so prized. *Mesta* horse descendants.

But where this gangly, gigantic, Percheron-looking, white, flea-bitten horse came from no one I knew remembered, but he was a free-ranging celebrity in a way all his own.

Because nobody claimed to own him, and the little semi-wild tribal horse herds that wandered all the open land surrounding the village wouldn't allow him in their company, this gelding lived a pretty much forgotten monastic life. People would spot him now and again, usually along the east side of the river, in the cottonwood bosque. But sometimes he'd show up twenty miles off, or so, over on the surrounding low mountains.

Well before it was time to plow, tribal officials would appoint a mounted group to search for him with orders to try to catch him and bring him into the corrals. They'd proceed to hitch him up and people who knew how to plow with a horse took turns plowing each other's chile plots. He was really good at the kind of plowing that the people's corn and chile demanded because they irrigated their fields with an antique Spanish method using the water off the Rio Grande in an old-time "pre-American" patterning that a tractor couldn't exactly approximate.

When the last farm along the river had been plowed and planted, this old horse was handed over to the tribal group in charge of mustering and branding all the spring calves. A large, old driftwood holding-pen lay alongside the river's edge. This was employed during the general rounding up of mother cows and their babies brought in to brand from the hills off the west side of the river, where they wandered grazing in thousands of acres of open land. Assigned riders, on those special little Native horses, would spread out in pairs across that territory full of deep ravines and steep, rocky hills returning with as many mother cows and their babies as they could find and drive them down off the hills into this corral.

Made of upright *sabina* trunks and driftwood jammed together and wired into a tight oval enclosure large enough to hold at least four hundred cows or more was where the fires for branding had already been lit and the old men smoked and waited patiently with the hot marking irons.

All the kids sent out to gather cows wanted to ride the gigantic white horse, for—though he was hell to catch and took three people to hold him still enough so you could get on without getting thrown—once you were settled in the saddle, he drove himself. He was big, fast, and smooth and felt like riding in a limousine, but unlike most horses his size he could turn like a hummingbird and knew exactly what his work was. The strangest thing about him was he didn't want any interference from all kinds of superfluous signals from the rider, who was just there to let him know that there was work to do, not to tell him how to do it.

No cow could turn and get past him, no calf would dare to bolt or even try to outrun him and the best thing was you didn't have to do anything to motivate or turn him because he did all of it automatically! No matter how bad a rider you were, he made you look like a pro, just as long as you could stay on. As soon as all the cows and calves that the riders had been able to find had been brought down to the fires and the branding began, this old horse was at his happy best. He would rule the branding yard, singling out the calves, holding them tight for branding. Everyone vied to be the one sitting on him. He was the one that really taught me how to stay put in the saddle and to predict a horse's next move.

Because we kids hadn't mastered the art of calf-roping from the saddle, like you see in the rodeos or the movies, the middle-aged men on the ground would wait till this old gelding, deftly jumping back and forth, had singled out one eligible calf. Then like a parent taking their kid to his first day at school, this nameless old horse would bring the scared baby cow over to the older men and drop him off, where they'd very gently drop a rope over the calf's head or his two hind legs, while another man quickly handed the other end of the rope to whoever was riding this amazing all-purpose horse. These ropes had a special little loop braided at the end and all the rider had to do was drop that loop over the saddle horn and, being careful to keep his fingers out of the ropes way, wait for the horse, who would then by old custom, at just the right moment, step back or sideways away from the roped calf, gently tightening the rope, drop him and stretch him out, while two men grabbed his head and hind, held him down, and a third put the tribal mark with hot irons to the calf's left hip. If there was an earmark, somebody did that. If it was a bull calf they were branding, they castrated him with a sharp pocket knife, then doused the wound with wood ashes and went to roast the testicles in the fire, which the men ate with stewed chiles, big homemade flour tortillas, and boiled coffee that their wives and mothers had delivered.

Except for heating and applying the hot irons, all the boys and men, regardless of age, took turns doing the different parts of all this and by the next day we kids were so stiff we could hardly roll out of our sheepskin pallets. That old horse, on the other hand, was totally undented and ready to do anything put to him. Once all the plowing and livestock marking was completed, the old, nameless, white horse was released to fend for himself until the following year. That was his life, year in, year out, until it was presumed he had finally died. But to be truthful, his demise was never verified: he just disappeared.

I was so surprised later on, after having left the states and returned, to read and hear people routinely talking in such broad generalities about horses: that horses are like this; or that they always did that; or erroneous platitudes, like a galloping horse will never run over a person; and so on.

The only thing for sure about horses is that there is nothing for sure about them. They have individual souls with very individual, non-general quirks that are in no way the same as any other. They are all unique. I often wonder why horses as an everyday transportation were so thoroughly and quickly abandoned at the onset of the so-called advancement of the modern machine age. I'm sure it must be because they are not machines and no believable manual can be reliably issued for dealing with all horses, like could be done with obedient machines, made like cookies on an assembly line.

When I grew up, "the owner's manual" of any horse was the owner's experience with the horse. People think horses can be hammered into a user-friendly shape, but most horses have personal quirks that have to be anticipated, if not ironed out. You mostly just had to roll with it all, or walk. There was no such thing as a breed or horse that did this and didn't do that, like a brand of automobile.

How that old, nameless, white horse came to develop all those uniquenesses was unknown to us all, probably from some life of his from another place, but he was so useful that no one ever complained about his weirdnesses, they just learned what they were and went with it. Otherwise, he'd be gone in a second.

It was odd in a way, that a horse that well known and appreciated never had any kind of a name and no one to feed him something special or check his teeth or trim his feet. So there's no wondering, why just like a lot of very pampered horses in tight little stables, that this horse, who after roaming the world at will for at least ten months of every year of his life was almost impossible to catch. It was a yearly challenge for whoever or whatever group was put officially in charge of finding and catching him, sometimes even taking weeks just to find him and then another week of strategy to get a *mecate* over his head. But once he was saddled and mounted he was calmer, more capable, and more conducive than any horse I've ever known since.

So, it came as no small source of surprise and comic admiration when as a kid, I, of all people, turned out to be the only one who could consistently catch this big, prized, underfed, nameless, semi-feral horse with ease. Using a bizarre method that seemed not only to work every time, but one in which you didn't have to really search; he just came looking for you right of his own free will! When you got down to it the horse told me his secret himself.

We had all been saddling him one spring, along with the

other guys' beautiful little Barb horses, to go search for cows and calves, when I noticed him following me about, practically knocking me down trying to get a sniff of my breath. Everyone knows how much horses like to read the odoriferous messages written on their butts and breaths, especially horses that have just shown up. But this nameless wonder's nostrils were attached to my mouth as if he was here caught on a fishhook.

It was my turn to ride him in the branding, so I got up on him and went to work looking for cows. But later that night, as I dozed off, the memory of this nameless creature's strange attraction to my breath had me wondering if it was a secret I had discovered: that horses actually liked to eat *fish*! Because my breath had been full of the smell of some trout my father, brother, and I had caught and fried before I'd come to help the guys with the cows.

So I kept that thought to myself while another year of beautiful Pueblo life ran its seasons until the following spring when, as it turned out, nobody could seem to even locate, much less catch, this unnamed, big, old, white horse. People thought he was dead. I didn't believe it.

My mother had grown up in and around Detroit and though I'd grown up in New Mexico, our family had wonderfully varied culinary customs ranging from the steady local diet of red/green chile lamb, or pig, or deer, or elk, or beef, *posole*, beans, flour tortillas, corn mush, rabbit meat stews, fried *chimaja*, prune pies, along with all the buns, cakes, dumplings, cookies, lasagnas, spaghettis, macaronis, cornbeef and cabbage boiled in milk, casseroles, roasts, chops and potatoes, bread, rice, salads, and of course the sandwich of the American Midwest. My mother's propensity for ornate and creative sandwiches were well-known but utterly foreign to the Reservation of that time. But she was a dedicated sandwich eater: braunshweiger and garlic sandwiches, egg salad sandwiches, cucumber and garlic sandwiches, onion sandwiches, ham and cheese sandwiches, and BLT sandwiches, etc.

But her all time doubtful sandwiches, as far as all the Indians were concerned, were the tuna fish salad sandwich, the sardine sandwich, and the anchovy paste sandwich. My mother's sandwiches of canned fish from the sea made all my sidekicks squint their eyes and want to puke. Though they were a fascination to some, these fish and mayonnaise sandwiches were considered inedible by all. But a plan to catch this big, white horse had taken a rough form, so I asked my mother if she could make me four tuna fish sandwiches, American style.

All the women on the Reservation were tremendous bread bakers, baking beautiful loaves of Spanish white bread in their *hornos*. My mother's bread was also of the best and real home-baked, mom, white-bread, or rye, or black bread would be her normal holders for all the outlandish garlic slathered fillings she loved. But when I asked for Wonder Bread, she looked at me stunned and devastated. Then she stared and scowled.

Then she laughed and knowing me pretty well figured that I must've had something up my sleeve and went ahead and made me four regulation American tuna fish sandwiches with Wonder Bread and mayonnaise expertly wrapped in wax paper (before the scourge of the invasion of plastics), all with a minimum of flinching.

After hitchhiking the five miles from the school compound where we lived to the Pueblo, I borrowed a rope at a friend's house, then sauntered through the village down to the Big River (Rio Grande) and once over the bridge jumped off the dirt road and headed south for a mile or so through the bosque of cottonwood all boggy with the snow melt of spring.

I sat myself up onto the massive trunk of a toppled cottonwood. I'd seen horse tracks thereabouts in the mud and since they were big ones I surmised they must have belonged to the nameless wonder horse.

I laid three of the sandwiches alongside of me on the barkless, sun-bleached trunk. In the clear air of spring and the smell of budding trees along with the delicious mud and rank-low-toned-stench of last fall's rotting leaves, the smell of fish was redolent and distinct.

As I started to eat the first sandwich, by the third bite and still chewing, right in front of me in the south surging river, a big white head came floating, like a gigantic beaver, heading straight toward my riverside perch.

Emerging from the water, pulling himself up onto the bank, the big white horse shook off the water like a dog and with the spluch, spluch, spluch, spluch of a horse walking in wet leaves and liquid mud, to my great delight, he came trotting directly to my sandwiches, mud flying everywhere.

With all fifteen hundred pounds of him crashing straight toward where I was now standing, with the rope wrapped around my waist, I hid two of the sandwiches and held the third out towards him.

Like a ship sidling into the tires on a harbor dock, the big white horse rolled up against the downed trunk with a thunk and craning his powerful neck over it to get a whiff of the tuna sandwiches, surprised me by chomping off a big chunk out of one I was holding and swallowed it!

Holding what remained of the sandwich just out of range, I started walking sideways to the west. He followed me like a mosquito, until both of us were soundly inside the horse impound on the west-side branding pen.

I gave him another sandwich while I closed the gate, then slowly slipped the soft, worn, grass rope over his ears and fastened it around his neck while he chewed. And there he was, painlessly caught by the means of a tuna fish sandwich.

Nobody had seen it happen. So I was able to keep my secret for a couple of years, until I finally caved into the badgering of my sidekicks and thereafter it became common knowledge that to catch this sixteen and a half hand, white, farming and cutting horse you had to have four tuna fish sandwiches!

As to the question as to whether horses eat fish or not, this particular horse most certainly looked forward to a fish sandwich. He might have completely disappeared from the world, no one having seen him for weeks or months, and if you showed up on the river with tuna sandwiches there was no need to even search, he'd eventually appear, drawn in by the smell of the cheap school-kid lunch on the wind waiting for him in the riverside forest. It always worked. It became part of tribal knowledge.

Where he came from we could never ascertain. People searching for him over the wide land found his tracks here and there, but following them, they always lost them at the river. They might find tracks again in the mountains, but nobody ever successfully found him by tracking. There were very few who had the patience or luck to find him. But the odd thing was whenever he came to my tuna fish sandwiches he always arrived out of the river, his head appearing first, like a crocodile, his eyes and nostrils just above the water's level, paddling as some horses do in water, assiduously and expertly crossing the river, pulling himself out dramatically, kind of scary looking in a way, his bright white body glistening, big drops of water exploding off him like shrapnel in every direction.

I never saw him enter the river or drop into the wide river from the east side opposite. It was as if he was of the water, living hidden from view for months and when he felt like it he surfaced to eat fish sandwiches, generously plow our fields for us, chase, cut, and rope cattle for us and then, once released, went back to his underwater kingdom to resurface occasionally to check out how we were doing. Maybe he was a spirit horse, some kind of magical water horse that ate fish. He definitely ate fish and disappeared at will, was ridable without cues, and when he did come, he came out of the Rio Grande to eat tuna fish.

* * *

A lot of people, mostly people living for millennia along certain of the world's coastlines have, until the age of Euro-centric rationalism, been told in stories by their elders and by generally held belief, that their horses, originating a long time ago, were a gift sent ashore by the Lords or Ladies whose substance is the Ocean. For a lot of old time people horses did not come from the land; they came from the Sea.

The Irish Celts have any number of stories of how the first horses of Western Ireland were wild-maned surf waves that turned into horses as the waves hit the shore. These were the magical horses used by heroic beings in a time before our own and who thereafter formed the original herds of short, wild Irish horses whose descendants still roam the same coast today.

The continental Celts had the same experience. Their horses all coming from the sea at present-day Compostela or Marseilles becoming the brave, chariot-pulling, little horses whose drivers and woad-covered passenger-warriors were so terrifying in battles against Roman military and Greeks alike.

The ancient North African Berber people said their horses came out of the sea. The Soninke of West Africa, Guinea, Gambia, and Mauritania know that both their musical instruments and horses came as a single event, pouring magically out of the surf, ridden by magical people and that their koras were actually magical musical horses risen from the Atlantic. They say the horses of their powerful desert kingdoms were the sea come inland to be ridden by those famous sub-Saharan knights of the Kingdom of Ghana.

The island peoples of Indonesia, Malaysia and the Philippines have always recognized great dragon-like water deities with horse heads, manes and tails: dragon horses, the deities of the Sea.

Ancient Greeks, a slave-owning amalgamation of sea going, pirate peoples, if there ever was one, knew Poseidon, their Sea King, was the originator of all the great land horses, including Pegasus, the horse whose very traveling over the earth in service to Zeus has left footprints, which today form a series of steady water springs extending at least nine hundred miles across Europe and Asia Minor. These springs are the stopping and watering places of the great traders' migratory route during those grand eras that brought original horse-riding, Indo-European nomads into the Europe that is named after them.

The Caspian Sea was the origination of the magical Abghaz, Circassian, Kabardy, and Ossetian horses, as well as those of a number of Persian nomadic tribes.

And most romantically, out of the Black Sea, in a hundred tales have come the magic horses of the Old Russian Sea King, as well as the Hungarian Underwater Goddess, Daughter of the Sun, who had the Sun's Horses. No doubt the parallel births of both heroes and horses of the Scythian and Proto-Scythian Indo-Aryans, came straight out of the Pontus onto the Crimea into Central Asia.

The Buryat received horses out of Lake Baikal and indeed the enduring, little, woolly Yakut horses, whose fur is spun into yarn and blankets woven, do literally—in some way— emerge from the Arctic Sea.

One of the greatest mysteries of horses, if not the greatest, is the fact that while Africa has indigenous animals of almost every type—in particular humans—outside of indigenous asses and zebras, there is no evidence that Mother Africa had indigenous horses.

Today, there are definitely African horses, of course. But, we are not speaking of those Arabian horses of Egypt and East and North Africa brought by Arabs during the 7th century Muslim jihad or those horses brought by 18th and 19th century European colonial invaders in Namibia, Angola, South Africa, Kenya etc., or those Mongolian derived horses brought from Java by traders in *dhows* and traded inland to become the fine horses of the people of Lesotho today.

But, there are horses much older than these, descendants of ancient Asian horses in Ethiopia, Sudan, Algeria, Libya, Mauritania, Morocco, Senegal, Mali, Guinea, Gambia, Benin, Nigeria, North Cameroon, and Nigeria. These horses came to Africa some eight to ten thousand years ago with "their" people and are genetically Asian horses, not descendants of European prehistoric horses.

There is in vogue among some scholars an only slightly archaeologically evidenced conjecture that all of these horses arrived in Africa with their human tribal constituencies by way of the sea in a cultural phenomenon called the boat people: a sea faring people originally from somewhere in Central or North Asia, who also brought millet, yams, cassava, cattle, sheep, and goats to East Africa and horses and wheat to North and West Africa. To further this mystery, the original horses of Iberia, Spain, Portugal, and Southern France, that became so prized all over Europe, all descend from these North African horses and are not descendants of the indigenous European ponies or the heavy draft horses of the lowland swamps. Forming a landrace in Africa, these Asiatic horses of some earlier boat people became the famous Spanish Barb horses in demand all over crusader era Europe and after.

Most horse experts, trying to place this appearance of North African, Barb-like horses in Europe, want this phenomenon to correspond solely with the Arab-driven Moorish takeover of Spain beginning in the 9th century, and running for centuries, when most certainly a lot of good Berber horses poured into Southern Europe. But, even before Hannibal marched through with good little Numidian horses, no doubt adding to the goodness of the mix, before the Phoenicians, and a couple of thousand years before that, Spain had North African horses.

So, probably Spain and Africa initially received all these special, fiery ancestors of the Barb horses from Asian lineages in the same era, the same way: by boat. From where and who is hard to say exactly. But by sea it was, thus corroborating all the widespread folk stories of horses arriving anciently from the ocean.

Imagine how incredible it must have been to be sitting on the misty Galician shores shucking clams when all of a sudden a small horde of beautiful animals your people have never seen or heard tell of, come swimming out of the tossing sea, pull themselves ashore, their flying manes tossing like the foaming surf and running straight toward you to become the genetic center-post of all your people's native horses for ever more.

The people sailing these ancient ships in the olden times could not beach their craft with a load of horses without capsizing in the shallow surf. Instead, almost universally, sailors bringing horses by ship, in some places even as late as the 19th century, still jumped their horses off the decks into the sea and forced them to swim ashore from the anchored ship. This also accounts a good bit for the relationship between many ocean-going ship cultures and horse cultures. Since very ancient times, and still today, the knots and gear of horse cultures worldwide have a synonymity in both the religious and practical use of the exact same knots still in use on the decks of ships, especially sail ships.

In some places horses were even herded by people in small boats, swimming from island to island to change grazing and to gain a new gene pool with fresh stallions from other island herds. Horses and boats are a together thing everywhere. It is still known how certain of these widely distributed small Asian horses, in particular among certain Celtic peoples, subsisted by eating seaweed. The horses like their coastal cattle, could also handle flesh from the sea if dried and pounded, to avoid bones in the case of fish and shells in the case of mollusks.

Even in places where the people may not have seen an ocean—and where horses though prehistorically present had disappeared, like in the interiors of North and South America, before being re-introduced by invaders—Native Americans knew their horses were something Holy, fierce, and a gift from beneath the surface of revered waters of certain rivers and pools throughout their territories. Native peoples of

North America all have under water Gods of varying types of physiognomy and custom: In the American Southwest (Pueblo people, Taa Diné, Apaches), in the Plains area (Cheyenne, Arapaho, Shoshone, Comanche), in the Southeast (the Chahta, Chickasaw, Euchee), in the East (the Leni Lenape, Haudenosaunee), up North (Ojibwe Canadian, Cree), to name just a few. All these peoples have tribal story-memories where some species of a spiritually powerful water monster surfaces as a foam-maned Water Horse.

⚫ ⚫ ⚫

So, when we continually saw our white-maned horse-friend coming to us, always surfacing from the river, to eat our fish sandwiches, to help us to work the fields—as water does plants, to bring our animals home—to help the people have meat, we knew that this fish-eating Water-Horse was none other than the spirit of the substance of Water Herself come to give us life.

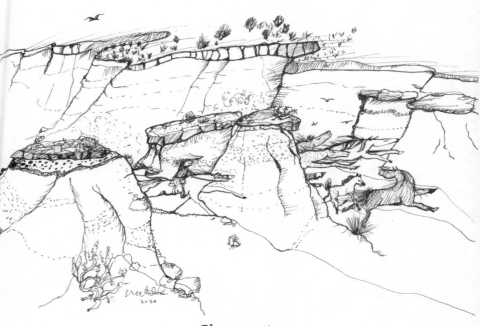

Chapter 5

Canyon Wren

As a child and into my teenage years there were certain sounds of both the natural world and the sounds of people that were emotional vitamins to me.

Sounds of baby skunks, wild-sounds of sand polishing cobbles in the tree-snapping wind.

Sounds of three hundred wild doves in unison marching in a sandy desert blow out.

Sounds of tree crickets and black crickets all night, all summer.

Sounds of fluffy snowflakes making their tiny sound as they piled flake by flake, inch by inch, foot by foot.

Sounds of the Pueblo evening's children yelling at a *shinny* game five miles away in the spring.

Sounds of the rumbling hooves of sixty horses rushing past our house every couple of days.

Sounds of feral cows snapping at late summer's flies with their ears, as loud as fly swatters.

Sounds of big, grumpy, bumblebees and quiet, tiny, green, metal bees sharing the pollen on blanket flowers.

Sounds of migrating cranes and flushing quails.

Sounds of rocks as they wake up to the sun.

There were so many more.

But of all the sounds, it was the sounds of birds that most dependably fed the soul: like the shy mumbling of bluebirds, juncos, siskins, grosbeaks, goldfinches, towhees, and other birds whose songs were the voices of the snows and needed to be there for it to be winter.

Or the sounds of birds that belonged to the cooling-abalone-evening sky, where after a day of shimmering-rock-melting-summer heat, the timid beauty of their symphonic alabaster tinkles, so distant and almost vague, everyone knew was the offering that might make the rains agree to finally come.

But of all those birds whose songs gave me life, there was one I could never manage to set my eyes upon, and whose name for years I failed to discover in any language, but whose song, mightier than all the others, rang only up in the steepest walls of the stony ravines that ran for miles beyond the Big River to the west. Canyons said to be owned by a species of Holy Giants who watched over the bears and trouts and pines and creeks from caves just beneath the fir lined capstone. Caves and crevices out of which this bird's startling song burst forth, the echo of his voice cascading down the sides, driving the little canyon-cutting creek rippling out and away from the mountains into the Big River, past us, pushing the water all the way to the spiny oyster studded Sea of Mexico.

This bird was famous among Natives for singing only in the ruins and significant spiritual places of their ancestors. It was secret knowledge that this bird himself, not just his voice, was the mind of these powerful, beautifully-dressed Giants, who, from the unpeopled natural world surrounding the Pueblos, guarded their people. When you heard this bird, it was the speech of a specific Giant, whose voice was a bird, a voice not housed in the Giant's body, but in the wild canyons outside the Giant's body, as a bird.

His sound was not to be found just anywhere. You couldn't find the song by searching anyway. It could not abide the sounds of people's minds and if you showed up with noisy thoughts rattling in your head, the Giant's voice, this bird, would elude you. But once your mind was cleared and his song found you, its notes floated out and down off the cliff's edge that towered overhead, dropping straight into the deepest territory of your soul, and with or without your permission, rolled around inside you like an old cat in a flowerbed.

The song was always a surprise, the thrill of its friendly, unlikely sound bolstered the courage and stamina in a way that I'm sure caused the frail constitution of my early days to gain strength in every definition and direction, for the Giant's voice echoed inside me just like it did inside the canyons I was inside of when it came.

It was there in these same canyons where these great mythic beings lived. But mostly unseen, for the majority of these creatures lived asleep for centuries in caves. Everyone who had traveled to those places would report how they had heard the low rumble of their snoring deep in the stone, which you really could hear if you tried hard enough, something for which I can attest. Over the years more than one geologist has asked me about those low sounds in the Northern New Mexico ravines.

All people said, that all the old people had said, that these Giants were not to be disturbed or awakened by the impertinences of any nosy humans. But in any event, they would someday awaken when a truly big earth change was to occur, for which they would be the major orchestrators. But though their bodies lived by dreaming in their sleep, the Giant's voices nonetheless remained awake and roamed about at will seeming to us as birds whose song we can still hear in the Giant's canyons, who are the Giants talking in their sleep, monitoring the world and keeping the wild Earth safe.

In my adolescence it was this same magical sound, this bird's song, the sleeping Giant's voice, that regularly restored my well-being, my mind, my body. Even when the unnatural world of the "Empires" English-speaking, compulsory schools, with their impatience and dreary models of irrelevant, canned-chicken-noodle-soup progress, sadistic "teaching" methods and placebo, post WWII, air-raid drills forced me to harden up to hide the things I really cared about, feeling scared and irrelevant, wounded, cold and left behind, if I could just get out into those rolling unpeopled hills, up past the Big River into the red stone and black, glass-studded, tufa cliffs you met before the big red mountains of the Jemez rose up, then, even though my head was full of the rehashed, robotic noise of civilization's hurt, phrase by phrase, the Giant's bird-voice would descend to me from the cliff-top caves like a musical rope ladder, over which I could climb, step by step, note by note, up and away from all the banal soul-killing monstrosities of the day and slowly pull myself back onto the shores of who I really was.

● ● ●

But riding horses free and concerted over the wild land, letting the wind run through me to clear the irrelevancy of modernity's curse out of my innards was the next best thing, if I couldn't get to the cliffs twenty miles away.

Unfortunately, my family didn't own any land and my parents certainly owned no horses. Luckily, Pueblo families generous there were, with horses to share and with whose youth, we tore off in bands of six or eight straight up and through the rugged, unfenced beauty; sometimes coursing distances so far off that the bird would find us, our souls already blown clean, both riders and horses happy, panting with life.

After Gilbert broke his arm and he couldn't ride for a few months and he loaned me his wonderfully awake and energetic Cow Pony—a little, solid-red, reservation Barb of the old *Mesta* type—it became something of a regular pilgrimage for his little bay horse and I to ride out by ourselves literally flying over the shrine-covered hills, every hoof beat hammering my frayed soul closer back into the saner stratum of the atmospheric bark that lay closest to the real Earth herself, to a place where I could finally shed the husk of the weird person all of us had to adopt to survive the New Mexican version of the white men's hand-me-down school.

If Gilbert's horse and I were fortunate enough to have ridden that way, far enough into the Giant's land, and his bird voice graced us with his song, then the echoing voice of the Canyon Giant would wash over us, horse and I, both still, standing, waiting, mane and hair blowing in the wind long enough until the bird's song was in my blood and by that I was made whole enough to ride slowly back home and try to be a person again, though never quite the person people wanted me to be.

By the end of the tumultuous confusion of what the 1960's meant in New Mexico, so much of the Indigenous life ways I had identified with had either evaporated into the tumult and confusion of the age, or those that had survived, were denied to me, when certain Native regimes understandably closed their mental and physical borders trying to keep out a world that the deep Pueblo order perceived as an even worse threat than the conquests.

Though probably justified in many aspects, a whole village of the only friends I'd ever known and the land herself stood sequestered behind that wall of new conservatism, intentionally held out of my reach. They would have to live in my heart and always have.

By my early twenties I wandered away from the United States trying inexpertly to outrun that extreme loneliness,

along with the simultaneous loss of my mother to some mysterious and untimely death, as well as the loss caused by my own
naïve attempt to remake tribe and family through a bad marriage during the unstoppable flood of the same middle-class,
Americanized mediocrity that had already culturally flattened
both urban and rural Indigenous and ethnic neighborhoods
in most of the other states. Up until then, New Mexico had
largely been spared. Some of its greatness and sanctuary for
a deeper human and natural magic would survive it all, but at
the time I couldn't bear the sight of what to me was the virtual
extirpation of all I believed in. So searching for life, looking
for home, I left, heading south, only because it was so easy.

This was in no way an organized journey with any intended aim or planned trajectory, but an attempt to outrun
sorrow. The trick, I felt, was to keep moving, to constantly
flee. I found, if I traveled and never settled, I could outrun
the heartbreak by a day or two, which by then, the excruci-
ating hurt would have caught up to me. Drawn off and away
by the marvels of Mexico I'd never seen but only heard tell,
rolling a bit ragged, with no money and no way out, no safety
net, I moved unknowingly through the Mexican states of Chi-
huahua, Nayarit, Durango, Michoacan, Oaxaca, and Chiapas,
along coasts in the sun, inland, on little snub nosed buses, on
foot, in the back of work trucks. For at least a year and a half
I was like a rolling ball disintegrating as it rolled, until I lost
momentum and all that was left of me was a small round core.
Like a lost bead from a broken necklace, I washed up onto
the black sand shore's rotting reeds and mahogany canoes of

Lake Atitlán, Guatemala where after a few years and peram-
bulations I became a citizen and member of Tzutujil Maya
society in the big Mayan town of Santiago Atitlán.

Life can be majestic when you get pared down to your
core, probably because small things mean so much then, as
they always should, but there is no way to express my delight
at being proved wrong about being forgotten or alone, for to
my great surprise, in all my wandering, no matter where I
camped or into whose generous hut or house I landed for a
night, in every place I slept, upon waking, there singing, with
all the same force, same lusciousness, and the same notes was
the bird I'd always known as the voice of the sleeping Giant,
the bird of the canyon of my youth. Everywhere I went he was
there. Close or far, one of those sleeping cave Giants saw what
had happened with me and had sent his voice to travel along
with me, keep me company, trying to sing courage and keep
magic alive in my broken heart.

The powerful Tzutujil enclave living in several villages on
the southern shores of Atitlán, when they took me in, was at
the beginning of its finishing days as a totally self-sufficient,
aboriginal, corn-farming, canoe-carving, fishing culture with a
highly organized spiritual hierarchy of both men and women,
adapted in some appearances to old 16th to 17th century Spanish
culture, but deeply embedded with the Holy unseen government of Nature resident inside all the mountains, valleys, and
the waters of the lake. It was here in Santiago Atitlán where it
was realized by one of this spiritual hierarchy, that I was a very
complete but badly assembled jumble of very good parts.

It was here where I was taken apart as an American and put back together again as a person. It was here I was allowed to become a Tzutujil. The price of this gift was my own continued service inside that same hierarchy, whose old citizens gave me life, and in that capacity I found myself at home and beginning to become a fairly competent caretaker of old knowledge and the oral mythic "blueprints" of the people's love of being themselves as the "spouse" of the Wild Natural Earth, as the stories put it.

And through all that, though this mysterious bird still gave us his song, I for one, in my entire life, had yet to set eyes on its shy author, until one day up on the side of the volcano of Atitlán, there he was. His beautiful curved bill, his short, hoppy, little legs, his brown body flecked with white spots, with other spots inside those spots, as if covered with a hundred eyes looking up and out quaked as the bill, wide-open, generated his wild cascading sunlight of sounds. Noticing the reverence that came over me when this little fellow sang, my middle-aged companion in our official duties on that junglely cliff began filling the day with the tale of the *Chajal Siguan*, the Guard of the Canyon, as this bird is known throughout Indigenous Guatemala, or the *Guarda Barranca* in Spanish. The conquerors also called him the New World Nightingale and he was so prized in the 16th century that one of them imprisoned in a cage was equal to a horse in trade!

Even more precious to the highland Indians, the Canyon Guard held a place of reverence that could not be purchased. For when this most recent world, the one we all live in today, was just starting up, and all was dark yet, and the Sun and

Moon just newly originated were unable to budge, though they had all the offerings that should have fueled their motion into the recently invented sky to kick-start the world into life for the first time, nothing could get them going. So a contest was set among all created beings, and all the Gods were called upon to summon each and every being known and unknown, so that each with his own particular magic would in turn try to coax, or push, or pull, or scare, reason with, or prod, or tickle, trick, or magically cause the Sun to get moving to turn eternal darkness into day. Every God, every animal, every weather, everything tried but all for nothing, because the Sun just sat there lazy, fat, and hot, eating the offerings unable to rise.

Finally, the soul of the Rock of the Canyon, inside of which this new Sun was created and enthroned and from which he refused to budge into the sky, appeared in the form of this little brown bird, the *Chajal Siguan*, the Canyon Guard. He said he would try to make the Sun move to make the first dawn come to light. So small, drab and innocuous, all the beings of the world started laughing at his presumption to be more capable than all of them and just dismissed him as a comedian.

But with nobody's say-so, he hid inside the canyon walls, inside one of the famous *Uqub Jul, Uqub Siguan*, those ancestral caves that lined the upper story of this famous ravine. Then this little bird's singing began, filling the inner labyrinth of the caves with his waterfall of sound until the world heard that the rock itself was singing back in harmonizing echoes.

With a windy-whistling-creak, thunder, and a terrifying rumbling, they say, the Sun without even willing it, commenced to rise up and out of the canyon, on the song. Setting the local woods on fire as he passed close to the rim, he threw his young light and fire over the not-yet-flowering earth, ascending somewhat violently into that same route he still follows now, as the first dawn flooded into day.

The inherent power and beauty of the little bird's first song was the voice of Rock Herself, to whose gravity the Sun's light and heat was not only subservient, but to whom the Sun owed his very existence, as his fire was only the male spark born of the female rock. Withdrawing from the rock into the sky by the thrill of the little bird's voice, the wonder of the Sun's day was directed and ecstatically inspired; for the Sun's movement to Mayans *is* time; the Sun's work *is* time and his work is heavy. So time is heavy. That heaviness, like rock, is only moved by the powerful feeling that bird's wild, natural music inspires, making the world happen. Therefore, the *Chajal Siguan* today is revered as the maker of every dawn ever since: the sound in stone that makes time mature.

When they saw how this little being had been able to do what they could not, all the world's myriad beings, all the contestants cheered, yelled, or sang out. This is why at every dawn, when the Canyon Guard sings, the Sun rises, and everything else begins to stir or sing its name: the winds stir, the waves on the lake slap, the water birds scream and rise and flocking resettle on the water; and all the animals scurry, the birds in all the forests and villages begin to chortle, screech, coo, or warble, each in her own form, all the people stir, make fires, cook breakfast and head to their daily work chattering like birds.

So to this day, because the *Chajal Siguan* can be heard every morning calling the day's new born Sun to crown like a baby's head out of the day-birthing, volcanic, rock thighs of his mother, the Wild Natural Earth, accompanied by a loud chorus of tropical birds, traditional Indian mothers when giving birth to their children in their huts were always accompanied by the relentless, breathy jazz of flutey bird-whistles blown and tooted by their neighbor's small children to call into life their new baby sibling or cousin to come in fully born. In this way every woman's child was the Sun, every birth a sunrise, and every little kid a Canyon Wren calling up the Sun. Every birth, human, animal, and plant was a miracle called into life by the Chief of All Birds, out of the ancient stone womb, by the Canyon Guard and his magnificent dappled array of birds. The Canyon Wren had followed me from the canyons of Native Pueblo Giants to the Sun-calling volcanic cliffs of Atitlán in Central America. I was not alone.

My years in the Guatemala Highlands would all be years without horse riding.

There were, of course, horses, mules, and donkeys in the highlands and a lot more truly awe-inspiring little horses in the Pacific coastal lowlands and the eastern desert cattle country. But like all the people, all of these horses were horses with jobs, not pleasure horses, not race horses, not horses for show.

Horses there were either in pack trains mixed with mules, driven by pedestrian *arriéros* between the highlands and depots on the coast, or as fate-defying tiny seven hundred pound horses ridden by very tiny, brave, barefoot men very capably balanced in beautiful, handmade saddles with undersized straw hats cocked sideways on their heads, who by a short rope could be seen dragging recalcitrant, two thousand pound zebu bulls to *bramaderos* on the coastal *fincas*!

But for the most part, except for the highly guarded, untouchable, wealthy elite, horses had never been ridden much, just to ride. This, partly because the land was all straight up scree fields, or straight down forests, and all other land was dedicated to mountain-side, terraced cornfields, making travel more suited to Indians on foot, or squirrels, deer, or monkeys. Not to mention, in those highlands, grass was scarce and there were no hay fields.

Though culturally rich, living was very basic in the mountains. It could cost more to feed a small horse than to feed a family of four, in which every member had to pull his or her own weight to survive, so a horse would be kept only if he could work more than he would eat or take time to care for.

Even so, Guatemala like all the other countries with large Indigenous populations, the residual effects of 16th and 17th century European ordinances enforced on their colonies, which, in the case of the Spanish, forbade any Native, excepting hereditary Indigenous kings and their families, the right to bear firearms, forbade them the right to ride horses, mules, or donkeys (they could pack them) and were forbidden as well the right to wear any kind of large feathers in their hats, or hats so tall that they might cause an Indian to stand taller than their foreign colonial overlords! (Another rationale for not allowing Indians to ride was that a mounted Native would place him at a height above his would-be superior on foot).

Designed to curb Native people from gaining the upper hand in the many cases of organized rebellions that all oppressed peoples resort to when life becomes intolerably insulting and difficult, these same prohibitions were intended to apply to all conquered populations throughout the colonial empire.

Indians in western South America had existing pack animals and a very sophisticated network of roads long before the European intrusion. But in a lot of Spanish over-run places like Mexico and Central America where the land is so close and heavily populated and under close scrutiny, Natives never got a taste for horse culture and maintained their sophisticated culture very ably on foot. This did not, of course, deter their colonial overlords from training Indians to become expert horse herders and packstring drivers to serve their own "master's" feudal-business transportation needs.

But in the areas now comprising Northern Mexico, Texas, New Mexico, Colorado, Arizona and California, with so many far flung nomadic tribal peoples, and spread out settled populations of Native village farmers, not to mention the free-booting mentality of many colonials who themselves were usually at violent odds with their own legal overseers, these laws became difficult to enforce.

Most of the nomadic hunting peoples became expert horse people overnight with newly organized horse cultures. Though Spain had officially banned slavery, in a lot of places designated as frontier, unsupervised Europeans had been illegally involved in intense forays to procure huge numbers of slaves from nomadic Native nations causing those tribes in turn to become "ranch raiders" in order to capture people to replace those lost to the colonial slavery. These "raiders" captured horses and herd boys in the process and became fierce horse cultures in one generation. To counter the effects of this new phenomena, the colonials, disregarding the law, armed their slaves and fief-held Natives and encouraged them to ride the very good Spanish horses.

Soon Indians everywhere in these areas had the best horses, developed unique gear, had the best saddles, and the best ability with horses, which in some places, New Mexico being the most prominent, contributed substantially to the so-called "peaceful settled" Pueblo people's ability to militarily drive their oppressors completely out of their country for at least twelve years in the famous Pueblo revolt of 1680.

In Guatemala, where earlier there had been a couple of equally determined and impressive Mayan revolts, none of these were carried out on horseback, but were more specifically designed to disable their armed enemies and destroy their horses with pit traps and other unmanned ambush techniques. For three centuries afterward the greater Indigenous highland population that remained survived as a series of able pedestrian cultures all of whom in my day still relied on their own strong backs and feet to carry out their agricultural and trade travel.

Regularly traversing incredible distances over the most challenging, unstable, and steep terrains, Native Mayan farmers and merchants often bore loads on their backs that would break even a horse's spine! And even those wealthy Indian merchants who could afford to regularly ride and transport their goods in the little communal Blue Bird buses that plied the two major highways running through those volcanic highlands between the bigger towns, upon arrival would still have to load up their merchandise on their backs and walk the remaining miles to markets in *aldeas* where often vehicle roads had not yet been engineered.

Earlier in the States, as a young person, like some of those anciently settled Natives turned nomad-horse-riding-hunter for whom the horse had been a way to get far away from colonial servitude and spiritual oppression, horses had been a way for me to escape from the "colonial mindset" I found so oppressive, still implicitly in place in the education system with its seemingly concerted campaign to invasively cheapen a culture's real depth, Native or not. The ability to ride horseback crazy-full-out in the endless, unfenced, wide-open Native terrain was a way for me, as a teenager, to keep alive my inborn epic nature in a land still full of ancient stories and unviolated mysteries. After all, spiritually undamaged horses, by their very nature, engender the love of mystery in the rider and encourage an almost irrational exhilarating need to do something difficult and worthy, something heroic; and they inspire a person to sing.

But during my twenties, during the late 20th century, in Guatemala—at least in the highland Mayan towns and surrounding "tribal" areas of the Cakchiquel, Quiche, Mam, Pocomam, Quekchi, Pocomchi, Uspantecos, Tzutujil and many others—

the people for all intents and purposes still lived as fiercely independent, beautifully dressed, exuberant, unmechanical corn farmer's in a kind of medieval, non-scientific time-bubble whose antique agricultural economy and mythological-minded royal Native Mayan language forced them to speak, think, and react in a truly everyday epic fashion. None of it was an act. It was very much in place, very ancient but always fresh, culturally rich, full of natural hilarity and wonder, with an intrinsic self-sense of the nobility in every person, at least among their own people. It was in every way copacetic with the spiritual specifications of the natural workings of my soul.

Balanced on the unruly backs of the corn-colored reservation horses of my youth, a real inner form had begun to gestate in me, mysteriously forming an epic self-culture from some innate sense of courage and honorable service to something worthy that humans must by nature have been always truly inclined, but largely lost now in the present age.

Though horses of the right salt and wild-wind can so thoroughly cause a kind of primal sanity and pride to surge up in one's blood, flying over the wild land in tune with your horse's mad smile can also give the sensation of actually being able to out distance the soul-numbing monster of modernity's disposable mediocre life.

But in those days, while held in the Umbilicus of the World, as the Tzutujil called their home town, I no longer needed such a horse to maintain the presence of an epic sense of life, for everything, every day was epic, the entire village rode the back of a mythologic life where the epic, the absurd, and the magical was in every person's thoughts and action, every spoken phrase, every motive, every disturbance. Life itself was epic. So, for me, there was nothing to outrun.

There was nothing to get away from, no need or desire to escape the village to find my own inner form. For in that village, it was expected that I would, in the normal motion of life, kind of "melt" into the form they defined as a real "person". Something everyone did, a form for which there was no equivalent in the modern condition. It was not a matter of everyone loving you or even agreeing with each other. It was like nature, where every animal and plant, weather and land-form belonged in the whole, whether friendly or not. I was respected, just as much as I deeply respected the mythic rhythm of our village. I felt at home and the village was at home with my being there, as if I'd always been there.

So, my time in Atitlán was horseless because I never need-ed a horse to outrun an ugly life, or to put me back together again, neither did I need a horse to bring me back home. I was already home.

The fear of not being able to "escape" wasn't there. That obvious need for mechanically supplied speed and motion to flee, that the modern person fears to live without, comes from an ironic, restless need for motion toward a better place. The modern person is only at home looking further and further afield for home, destroying everything it leaves in its wake, which movement disguised as progress, of course, never arrives home.

I had so little intention of "getting anywhere" that I wasn't already at, that for a decade and a half I didn't even drive a car, practically forgetting how. I spoke English only twice. None of this is to say I didn't miss horses, for I surely did. I missed horses, but I didn't *need* horses to find myself, because *I* wasn't missing. So like the entire population who walked everywhere, both together and alone, I walked everywhere, together and alone, but belonging everywhere I walked. We lived very well. Though often poor, in very harsh conditions, we lived beautifully, we were at home, and my old companion the Canyon Wren sang the Father Sun up every morning.

I would have never left.

But then the wars came.

For centuries, life on the edge of Lago Atitlán had been safely hidden in a long-lived, beautiful spell, in a gigantic, adaptive Indigenous dream in which every Indian since forever had been meticulously living out his or her inherited part; a dream that had cell-like absorbed, incorporated, and indigefied all visitors and invaders alike, never losing the original, mystic recipe of Tzutujil enchantment. In a dimension that mainstream America would never have, or recognize in others, my life in Atitlán was as a person pushed into the river of their dream, expecting to drown, but finding instead I could not only breathe and thrive there like a little, purple lake-crab, but from which dimension, when perceived from within the river bottom was actually a village of intense, laughing, cloth-weaving, corn-farming, fishing Mayans. While tourists and ethnologists boated over us on the surface trying to fish up tribal secrets, we all lived and loved right under their noses in that antique bubble of real, daily, mythic magic. But like a long lived galaxy that would finally lose all its stars, it had been a magnificent dream in whose river of ancient-story-water we lived immersed, but one in which the Tzutujil and myself with them would watch evaporate away, leaving us all gasping for breath, as fish out of water.

In the early 1980's, shaken awake, we would all meet the unabsorbable, cold-living-nightmare of the modern world's rude, unbeautiful tyranny face-to-face in a war that looked as if the country was dedicated to killing itself off.

Killing was everywhere, on every road, bullets, blades, bombs, prison, torture, everyone was scared, nothing was clear. All trust was gone. The grandeur of the Native was evaporated and the people stopped being themselves. Their culture became a living artifact, the people, plain-old citizens of Guatemala.

The ancient dream had fled inside, the beautiful spell was lifted, everything changed, nobody was at home, including myself.

The long, nerve-wracking tale of the heartbreak and peril of leaving Guatemala as a hunted leader with a Tzutujil wife and two babies to land camped at the base of the southernmost cliff of the American Rockies, in the ravines of northern New Mexico's wild forests, has been elsewhere written. Let it suffice to say that it was the shock and grief of losing the precious reality of having once been truly at home among real human beings that drove me back into the territory of my youth, this time far away from people, back into the bush, to the Gods, to the Holy in Nature.

And, of course, once again I was hoping for horses. Horses to bring me back home again.

Chapter 6
Icicles

From an opening in the thick ring of scrub oaks guarding the base of a cliff of sandstone shelves that rose in thick layers of petrified weathered cake like a tiramisu of blue clay shot through with invertebrate fossils, our tiny ten by twelve, unfinished cabin of massive, rough-sawn, fir planks, a timid three courses high, tried, but failed to peek out.

Down closer to the creek, from the doorways of our camp of tents and our tipi, when we left off slurping our morning tea, held our breaths, and strained our ears, we could just make out the song of the Canyon Wren modulating in the breeze of that April dawn. At least a mile up from us, on the ridge behind us, the little bird's flutey descending whistle was clear, though barely audible, his sound was nonetheless a force that diluted the toxic sludge of the anti-people agenda that had been collecting in my broken heart. After so much loss in our lives, his sound bubbled strong enough to distill my hatred into tears, until both smiling and weeping I met the Sun's early light like the wren did and only then did I begin to call that canyon my new home.

The Canyon Wren, the *Guarda Barranca*, the voice of the Giants of rock ravines had once again followed me. The things I held in my head, no matter how brilliant or correct I thought they were, were not as important as the things in Nature that had always held me; for no matter how far I had wandered throughout the world or in my mind, the sleeping Giant's voice was still my companion, despite myself.

Of course he was not singing especially for me that day, any more than he was still trying to raise the Sun; for he kept it up unfailingly in three minute intervals way past mid-morning, all because of a mockingbird hidden near us in the oaks, whose hideously shallow pop-cover of the canyon wren's magical cascade of notes was so loathsome and insulting to the Giant's voice, that the wren felt it was only his duty to replace the beauty in what the other had soiled and disgraced.

Going on for hours, it was a war of audible jewels, where each warrior courteously held back while his opponent finished his volley, before he returned fire with his own insistent tune. Instead of killing, such a battle gave life, the two sides together, the sum of their opposition had an overall beauty that instead of casualties made the listening world its beneficiaries, including this poor, self-pitying human who this day was most certainly spiritually buoyed up by such an agonistic symphony of creative wits.

How I longed for a good mountain horse to ride up and into that untrammeled territory where those birds' force-field of sounds claimed the cliffs, caves, springs, and trees. Where moving a little bit more at home on the back of an animal who herself probably would always long for her own home in a herd she'd never known and most likely never find, but in whose nostril steam, brain-vapors, and the smell of sweat that rose off her backbone, I could inhale the medicine of her own powerful faith in the internal directive of belonging to the land her herd-searching hooves faithfully tread, and in that at least, with her together, have some complicity in the sanity of always heading home into Nature instead of my usual failed attempt to dodge the shallow goals of civilization by rushing-away-from-home-to-hide-in-a-forest-bound flight.

But that day, no horses did I have. With a family of four to sustain, basically refugees with a hand to mouth money situation, we had no way to have horses. So once again I walked. I walked the mountains, the creeks, the canyons. Following the voice of the Giant, the voice of the stone, the canyon wren, and it was as grand as it could be, considering. But thank God, at least I wasn't...... hiking. I hoped no one had seen me moving through the hills on foot and figured I'd been hiking! For if anyone had thought that what our people did when we walked gathering medicine in the hills, or making prayers to understand what permission the customs of the animals to whom we bowed demanded, or what offerings of beauty or voice the bodies living in the roots and stones needed to have or hear for us to have been allowed to pull and dig them was just some kind of a pastime, or an outdoor sport, "hiking" to get a "hit of nature to put us back together" so one could go back into that bubbling, people-packed wreckage they call modern life, that would have been too much for my pride. I would have rather had my bottom frozen to the ground in the camp and tended the fire 'till I turned to stone. For me, a horse would be freedom from a culture that needed to hike. Though most of the horsey people I ever saw riding in the bush were basically just mounted hikers, people too lazy to walk, riding horses to "get outdoors", to come back and take up where they left off in the very Empire I wanted to, but couldn't seem to avoid.

So, I never hiked. I always walked. When I rode, I was never trail riding or pleasure riding. Though I would ride someday on trails and always in the bush or across the wild land on one mission or the next, working for this or getting that together with my animal, riding to me would always be a spiritual obligation; it was a prayer in just how we moved across the land. But pleasure riding? Never. We didn't ride for pleasure; we rode to feed the Holy epic in Nature, to give pleasure to God.

But that day, horses had I none. So I walked. I walked and walked. I prayed by walking. I didn't hike or trail ride.

Maybe sixty or so people lived within twenty miles of us. That was too crowded for me in those times, so deeply wounded was I by all the death, loss, heartbreak, and betrayal of which people were capable. But some of these houses seemed to have a horse or two out in their corrals. Sometimes I pondered if one could ever find a kind soul amongst them, make friends, then, maybe borrow a horse. Then sobering my mind, I told myself, "you don't want just any horse, you're looking for *the* horse," and hoping that someday an animal might appear, I just kept walking. But I never hiked!

Probably the human habitation closest to us was a quarter of a mile off, up on the main asphalt road that ran along the creek, where a man who was only rarely at home had a couple of small batten-and-rough-sawn cabins: one of them a gallery for his art, the other his home.

A rambling jackleg, pole-barn corral backed up against both buildings festooned with old, beat-up whiffle trees, traces, wagon wheels, and porcupine-damaged saddle trees from earlier times.

Inside that corral and seemingly always in the same position, two horses stood: one a little red, the other a big yellow beast. They stood like props in the most uncanny, co-operative, photogenic fashion to add the final choreography to what was intended, no doubt, to give the impression of an old western homestead, which got its specs from Hollywood, and not the Old West.

We could never seem to run into its inhabitant and had only the vaguest surmises as to what he was like, having only seen him at great distance, and even then we knew him better by the truck he drove than by his person.

One of those balmy, dry June days, while walking mid-morning back to our camp along the creek from the west, dropping down out of the high mountains after checking the *Oregano de la Sierra*, around the last bend of the creek emerging from the forest, I came square onto Mr. Conrad Purdy straddling the little creek, facing upstream, grumbling, tossing stones around. He pumped up his mumbling rap to a raving rant when he saw me.

"I gotta lay a trap out for that woman, I'm telling you, she's busted up my dam for the third and last time," etc. and so on.

"What woman is that Mr., I'm sorry I don't know your name..."

"That ornery Indian chick you live with, she's been break- ing up this dam right here, that's who," and blowing out a blue puff of angry cigarette smoke, while waving what I took to be work-swollen hands, then seeing how non-plussed I was, put one of them out for me to shake:

"Conrad Purdy, that's my name."

It turned out that where a kind of tiny, natural spillway rolled out of what remained of an old beaver dam, this Mr. Purdy, in a kind of half-hearted attempt, had built a little di- version-dam of his own with boulders, sticks, and mud across the narrow creek to flood a low spot behind the rise where his cabins sat to grow a little grass in a tiny pasture to feed his old horses.

It was still all kind of beaver-like in a way, but way more clumsy, and I very much doubted Dolores would have worried much about it, at least not enough to wreck his project, even though the whole thing was not on his land anyway, but on the land we were care-taking and diminishing the water level in her goose pond. He was accurate about her being onerous, but how he knew, I'll never know. But when I surveyed the scene of the alleged vandalism, there was no mistaking the fact that a good sized mama bear and her two babies had made a party of digging up his dam. Probably the same mother bear who had quietly made her way into our tipi early one predawn morning while everyone except myself was still asleep, sauntered off with our enamel stew pot, stew and all, the bale clenched in her jaws. No doubt she was teaching her kids some necessary bear lesson by tearing up the dam. My wife was not this bear.

Deciding that at our first meeting, presuming to be so up-pity as to educate a man like Conrad Purdy, that it was not the terrible threatening presence of unwanted, pagan, half-breeds and south-of-the-border, Indian low-lifes who were attacking his good western American efforts to settle the west again, but joy riding bears, was not prudent.

Obviously, living out some bad, romantic, western novel, with a persona gleaned from the movies, Conrad Purdy's non-New Mexico, cowboy image demanded that he be the superior author-ity on the "outdoors", incapable of misjudging "Nature and Indi-ans", who would interpret any counter opinions from the likes of me as ignorance and contentiousness, since people "like us" were foreigners and didn't really belong in his neck of the woods, even though I was a New Mexican and he was a Californian!

So I played along and told him I'd have a word with Do-lores, which I eventually did, but I held back for a couple of weeks before I passed it on, knowing it would set loose exact-ly what it did, which was to make her so humiliated and rabid about the likes of him wrongly accusing her of something just intended to make her ashamed of the Central American Indian she was, that toting a big, old, grubbing hoe she rushed right up the creek and seriously obliterated his fourth dam beyond recognition. Then practically starting a war, she went straight to his house and yelled at him to make sure he knew it was her.

A week later Purdy made some lumber forms and poured a concrete dike into the little *rito*, which worked for about ten days, until the summer rains finally settled the issue by wiping out his dam, his pasture, Dolores's goose pond, killing a horse, two cows, and tragically a child eight miles downstream in a fierce mountain flooding that broadened the tiny three foot wide creek into a sixty foot, earth-ripping serpent that for four days totally rerouted the tiny stream, cutting new cliffs and banks, which after shrinking back to her original three feet across, now ran fifty feet further to the north making it impossible for Conrad Purdy to divert, even if he still had something left to water. I wanted to laugh but didn't dare.

This made it all the stranger and surprising when four months later Conrad Purdy, with his cigarette, whiskey, and spurs mounted on his big, sweet, yellow horse named Yella of course and his little designer cattle dog, rode into our camp in the late fall. Copying all the Marlboro man poses you could imagine, he asked to talk to me. He wouldn't come in, but without dismounting, uncharacteristically accepted a cup of our coffee (which was famous by then, from Guatemala, of course) from Dolores's hand, then asked me if I could care-take his cabins, feed his horses, keep the fires going, keep off the thieves and vandals for two weeks in December, while he was gone to warmer ground in California to sell his cowboy art.

Still mounted, with us standing around, after he'd finished his cup, and me thinking it out, he let out, "You could ride old Bucky if you want to while I'm gone, but I don't want you messing with old Yella here."

"Well, what do ya say friend?"

I had no idea we were friends, but I couldn't refuse. A horse had come. Right where we lived, right there on our mountains, and without really thinking it out, I agreed. I couldn't believe my luck.

Double riding, I rode back with him to his roadside gallery, cabins, and corrals and like he'd been my best friend since birth, he gave me the tour, showed me the locks, the keys, how much, where, when, the mail, where he kept the firewood, the saddles, all the tack, ropes, the hay, the water, and finally Bucky.

Bucky was the horse of Conrad's sad, fifteen-year-old, young son. A boy named Colt, with a blond flat-top-haircut and a plaid shirt, from a divorced marriage, who stayed with his father for a few days every month. Purdy loved his son in a cowboy sort of way, but his son thought his father was some kind of god and must've treasured their little times together.

This kid was not a tough little cowboy—but a sunny, wounded child—friendly to all and we liked him.

Conrad insisted that old Bucky was a buckskin horse, which is why he called him Bucky, not because he liked to buck; just like Yella was yellow, not a coward, all normal "cowboy" names. But this horse Bucky was not a buckskin, but an ancient, solid-red-roan, grade gelding about 14.2 hands who Colter had known and loved his entire life. With Colt mounted on Bucky and Conrad on Yella, we'd seen them off and on, at great distance, as they talked and rode slow up through the mountain trails around us.

Two days later in the evening when Conrad Purdy tore out in his big-old, Dodge truck, earlier than planned, it must've been to beat the storm, for it was already snowing hard here in the mountains. He didn't say goodbye or thanks, and nobody saw him go. He left no contact information, no telephone, no address, but he left the keys right where he said he would, beneath an old barrel in the barn full of the spent harness leather from bygone times that he cannibalized to make his Old West artifacts.

By morning the world was gorgeous with snow, our tents bent in from the weight, the firs and ponderosas, their boughs fully covered in the night, began to shed their loads at dawn; and the creek bubbling under an inch of ice and eight inches of snow, its muffled tales sang.

Everyone was happy with the snow and like a little kid on Christmas morning I could hardly wait to be riding up the forested ravines in the quiet of the mountain snow. In our tipi, huddled warm next to our miner's stove, I wolfed a hot breakfast of blue corn mush, red chile, salted boiled eggs, and black tea with milk and honey, then shuffled through the powder in the diffused light of the snowy morning up to Conrad Purdy's cabins and corrals. Once in the barn, I prepared to feed his old horses. Thinking to catch old Bucky, bring him into the hay shed, scrape off the snow, dry him off and feed him under cover, I dug out his saddle, bridle, and blankets and piled them next to the door.

But with the *mecate* dangling from my forearm, when I entered the corral, old Bucky was couched out on the ground, all four legs folded under him, his head up, eye balls glowing weirdly blue, wavering all about, his back quickly gathering snow.

His breathing was halting and shallow. I cleared off the snow and tried to listen at his gut to see if he was colicking, felt for his pulse under his jaw, but it was distant. He was going cold and I knew this old horse was dying. If he'd been my own, I probably would have shot him to save him the hardship and long suffering he seemed to be facing. But he was another man's horse, put into my care, and if I shot him now maybe they'd think I hadn't tried hard enough to save him. So, I got on Purdy's phone and tried to find a vet, though as expected, it was a long shot finding one who'd make the fifty mile journey in the storm.

I thought if I could warm the old pony I might somehow be able to bring him back. As I covered Bucky with warmed blankets, old Yella stood watching, icicles forming from his dripping belly, his frozen nose hairs tinkling in the quiet snow-fall.

By the time the vet arrived two hours later, Bucky was on his side flailing on the ground. I'd put a bunch of folded saddle blankets under his head to save his beautiful, old eyes from being bashed out while he thrashed about. He was suffering bad and I so wanted to shoot him, but held off.

"Well friend, Purdy's old horse is dying. Conrad must've known it all along, that's why he took off so fast to leave you to handle it, so he wouldn't get stuck in the storm. I've known old Bucky here for a long time, he's very old, at least thirty or more. The best thing we can do for him is to put him down 'cause in this storm there's not much more can be done, even if we could get him to a facility, he'd most likely never make it anyway. It's a shame, really. And it's a shame you got stuck with having to make the decision, but that's my professional opinion. It's up to you to decide."

Reminding the vet that the toxic injections commonly used to put horses to sleep so they die painlessly and the chemicals used for euthanizing an animal that big would not only kill the horse, but also kill, or make chronically ill, or make infertile any bird, mammal, dog, cat, or insect who would ingest the remains of an animal killed that way, or kill any animal that in turn ate them, all necessitating that the remains of an animal killed this way be cremated or more irresponsibly buried, in an attempt to prevent the carcass from polluting the world. Most people just sent the remains to a dump. It was all too obscene. But the snow saved us from all of that.

The vet agreed with me that shooting the horse and then leaving Bucky's remains out in the hills to sustain the mountain's hungry wild animals would be the best route to take, given the situation, though we both knew he couldn't legally advocate that route. Besides which, in this blizzard any chance of burying Bucky's remains in the four feet of solidly frozen mountain earth was very unlikely and anything else impossible.

Unbelievable as it was, that after less than twelve hours of being in charge, the man's horse was dying. Bucky and I hadn't even really got to know each other and now his life was in my hands. I cradled his big, old furry head in my arms. And there I was, the same life-loving, naïve idiot I'd always been as a kid, who'd believed he'd finally have a horse to ride home into Nature's snow storm, and soon I'd have to say goodbye, when I hadn't even said hello.

Weeping and holding his head, I explained to old Bucky how I was going to sing him into the next reality, into the sub-molecular awareness, commending him to the Sun in hopes he would receive him as one of the horses of dawn's bright herd of stars. Then with all my might I sang.

I sang and I sang and I sang.

I sang until the old song finally made Bucky's breathing even out and he quit flailing and relaxed.

That was the moment I was hoping for; then still singing, I shot him through where the spinal chord connects to the brain, the bullet severing it, then crossing the cerebellum and exiting his left eye. The beautiful, old horse died instantly with barely a struggle, his last air exiting a moment later with a solid groan.

Like people, horses have more than one soul, that live in layers of history, in different parts of them. Some of those souls take a while to move on.

So, I kept singing until I felt at least his wind spirit was free, mostly off, and nobly dashing toward the Sun's herd of Dawn Star Horses.

With the loud, nerve-jangling bang of my old .30-30 still ringing in my ears, the redolence of the blue gunpowder smoke was quickly cleaned from the air by the snow, which now fell in clumps, like balls of feathers you could hear. Everything was silent now.

After a while, returning from his idling, warm, mobile-vet-truck, a little lost for words, the vet asked me how I'd learned to put a horse down in such a way, so cleanly, and so well, with no suffering. He'd never seen things done exactly that way. Shaking a bit and still very emotional, I probably told him too much. That it was part of an ancient way of being I'd been given as a young man from an old Pueblo Indian gentleman who had saved my life as an adolescent.

Though hampered by the storm and anxious to get to his next large-animal emergency some fifty miles off, the vet nonetheless stayed long enough to help me hoist the old horse's carcass onto my old truck with a cable-and-hook looped over a cottonwood branch pulled by a powerful, motorized winch installed on the front of his fancy rig.

With his hind legs dangling out of the bed of my old red truck, and Bucky's old, red, body fast gathering snow, alone, I drove him up as far from people as the heavily-rutted, unpaved, icy, mountain roads would let us pass without spinning-out or getting stuck and finding a high open place between the big trees, I lay him stretched out so the line from his head to tail was positioned toward the next dawn, so the rising Sun would claim him, according to old custom. Commending his body as a gift of welcome winter sustenance to be shared by all the amazing meat-eating, wild animals to whom people like me always bow their heads in awe and gratitude: to the mountain lions, martins, weasels, foxes, coyotes, bobcats, stellar jays, ravens, magpies, badgers, raccoons, skunks, hawks, eagles, squirrels, mice, and of course the bears, who were dozing underground busy dreaming this world into life with the meat-eating drone flies and bees, but whom one must never leave out, and the forest plants themselves, I drew out my always sharp little knife and took my own portion by shearing a handful of Bucky's red mane hair to later braid and give to Colter, this being the best I could do for his memory of his horse.

I wedged a turquoise bead into the dead horses clinched teeth, tied a shell bead in his mane, prayed again, and drove off, the old Ford slipping and fishtailing down the very cold, snow-packed mountain, before the storm's sudden increment into a horizontal blizzard would have had me hemmed in for good.

I brooded and worried as Conrad's two weeks turned into a month, at how I would tell him that I wasn't the reason his son's old gelding went down in the biggest storm of the decade, and what would I tell his son? Over and over I ran through all kinds of versions of weak rhetoric that always seemed too inadequate to the real situation. The vet, to forestall any possible misunderstanding, had generously written an extra-positive report to Purdy with his bill, exonerating any responsibility on my part for the old horse's mid-storm demise.

This was all complicated by the fact that even when Purdy took off, I was so excited to get riding, I made nothing of the obvious fact that the couple of bales that designer cowboy had left would be played out before even a week had passed, and now, even with only old Yella to sustain, I was already down three hundred bucks from buying over-priced bales, two at a time in Pecos, ten miles down the creek for six weeks. While this sounds like nothing today, in 1986 this was three hundred dollars we didn't have and I was forced to borrow.

So... when the weather eased up a bit in February, Conrad Purdy reappeared, all tanned and charming, driving a new truck, dragging a fancy, goose-neck horse trailer with a road-dazed, crayon-red gelding standing inside.

The roads were clear, but two feet of snow still blanketed the ground, the little stream was totally snow and ice covered with small breathing holes every forty feet or so, through which the flow could be seen very mystically. Of course everybody knows creeks breathe, because they are serpents of water, but only in winter does the snow show us where this serpent of water has her nostrils.

While I prepared to present the sad speech I had agonized over for the last month and a half, Mr Purdy, half yelled in an upbeat yodel, "How's it going kid, want to give me a hand unloading this old boy?"

It would've been hard not to notice that Conrad's speech patterns had started to morph from his original Bakersfield, California drawl into a drawn-out, west Texas, country radio sound.

After letting his new horse into the corral with old Yella, who didn't like this new addition one bit, and figuring that since Conrad would wonder why Bucky was absent, it seemed the time to let him know what had happened, so I began my speech.

"Conrad, I can't tell you in words how awful I feel about old Bucky dying in my care the very first day you…"

And with a wave of hands, Purdy cut me off and I got to hear more of his newly adopted accent.

"Why is it that guys like you git all the fun? Look, don't sweat it kid; its better you than me; I hate having to shoot a horse; and that way Colter can be mad at you instead of his Daddy; it's all just part of the game."

"Look here, you can ride this new guy if you want to. He's pretty young and won't go down on you like old Bucky. Anyway I gotta go for another two weeks, down to Austin, and try to sell my stuff. I'll be back as soon as I can. Go ahead and name the horse, I won 'em in a card game."

Still stunned by his response, I could only stand and watch as he dropped his trailer, opened the front door of his house, and without even looking around, grabbed his accumulated mail I'd piled there in a bucket, jumped into the driver's seat of his new truck, and unburdened by trailer and horse, dieseled west down the big highway at a pretty fair speed, once again, it turned out, to dodge the next set of snow storms.

Though Conrad never mentioned his feed bill and left no hay to feed the extra horse, for which I'd now have to borrow still more cash to feed, at least this time, he waved back at me as he fled.

Snow was once again upon us, but much heavier and wetter than before, causing impressive icicles to form, which hung thick from every available space, from every overhang, every tree bough, rolling over every snow nestled boulder until all the mountain sides and entire ravines glistened with icicles. Whole forests rattled and clinked in the breeze like a giant glass marimba whose wild noise at night drove all the dogs for miles to wail and made even the coyotes sing low, like wolves, accented by the groaning ice of the creek under the snow and the loud echoes of the popping of cottonwoods over-loaded with ice that split down the middle.

In the month of February, at the elevation of eight and a half thousand feet, the mountains of northern New Mexico, where the days were warmer than December and January getting all the way up to twenty degrees, the nights still got down to thirty degrees below zero, or colder. Keeping water thawed, animals fed, fires constantly stoked, drinking hot liquids, making every effort to stay warm and hopeful in our tipis and an uninsulated cabin was pretty much all we could manage.

Still chagrined and annoyed at myself, for having fallen so easily into his trap and mostly how much precious mental energy I'd wasted for six weeks agonizing about the feelings of a user the likes of Conrad Purdy, whose "art" turned out to be as a gambling, designer cowboy-con-artist, while we who struggled so hard just to eat and breathe, who not so long before and far away used to be respected chiefs and queens, artists, and weavers with land, positions, relatives and a real culture, who knew so much and had lost so intensely, were now just fuel for cruel jokes, laughed at for allowing ourselves to be exploited to maintain this man's "summer digs", all in keeping with what a certain social strata of unfeeling hate-filled types perceived as our logical station in life. After all of that, I was no longer in a hurry to exercise this man's new horse for him.

But it was very cold, and had been cold for months. I knew we had to keep our spirits up, to avoid the loss of immunity to sickness that sorrow, self-doubt, wet frozen clothing, and hopelessness causes in good humans already stressed. So, around a roaring juniper wood fire, I told the family slow, old, mythic stories every night, stories that were known to protect. I sang songs of the Holy Beings in the stories; I sang funny songs; and I told more old tales till the family dozed off a little less afraid, their relaxed breaths puffing white clouds of mist out from under their warm coverings. It was cold.

It was then that Bucky came in my dreams. He was in charge of magical dreams that prodded me back to my feet, out of my self-righteous doldrums and back into my original love of living, my love of snow, my love of horses, lions, and creeks and in love with the depth of my people, the music, the ground, everything. In his new form, which I only saw as I slept, what Bucky did with me in dreams, woke me up while awake. He put me back into myself. Like a good horse, he brought me back home to life through the cold snow storms that tore around outside.

Though his name had changed and his coat color more magnificent, it was him and no other, for when he showed up in my dreams he always spoke. The first time laughing in a joyful fashion, asking if I remembered the irony of what Conrad Purdy had said to me when he dismissed old Bucky's having died? "Better you than me," he'd said.

This new Bucky said he, himself, had arranged the hour of his death to make sure I'd be the one to properly sing him out old-style, into his next spiritual function as a natural horse, and make sure his form and body would also feed a multitude of powerful spirits through the devouring maws of the beautiful, hungry, winter animals. This new Bucky said his greatest fear had been to die stuck with Conrad Purdy when his time had come!

When still alive, he'd been a horse of the same, old-time blood of the *Mesta* that I'd grown up with on the Reservation, horses that had almost disappeared. He'd been an Indian horse from somewhere in Arizona scooped up in government horse clearances back when. Undervalued and characterized as a kid's pony by pseudo-cowboy idiots because, unlike the others, he turned out gentle and small. Having been lost in drunken card games more than once Bucky finally ended up with Conrad Purdy to even a gambling debt.

Horses are like water, in that most often they either become the shape of what confines them or react to it like a flash flood. But now, with no ignorant opinion to corral or limit his soul, this new Bucky, noble and powerful with his new liberty, decided he would let me "ride".

This new Bucky was a horse whose wind, water, and fire soul, unencumbered by any single physical form, could now jump into any living horse's body he so desired, until the time came for him to join the horse herd of the Sun, which are the stars of the morning that gather on the horizon when the Pleiades rises before dawn. So for the time being, his spirit identified so deeply with my situation, that he decided he would try to help us a little to live. Any horse I rode, he said he'd jump into and let me ride him until he joined the stars. He admonished me in one dream, "You'd better go ride that scared, vacant beast Purdy brought home the other day and then you can ride me because I'll be inside of him. I'll give you the secrets, you give me the ride."

Well, dreams are dreams, and once awake and surrounded by ice, its hard to tell how much to take to heart, but it wasn't likely that a person like me wouldn't listen to what a dream horse told me, so I braced myself and went ahead prepared to give it a try.

Conrad said I *could* ride him, the dream horse told me I *had* to ride him to receive his medicine for horses. Unless like a lot of stockmen in winter trying to save their starving sheep or cattle off stranded in the weather, where only an able horse could get to and you had no choice but to brave the bone-crushing cold, the deep ice-encrusted snow, the treacherous ground of ice, and the unpredictable bombardment of loud-ringing, horse-spooking, sharp, five-foot icicles crashing overhead from the trees, if you didn't have to, that particular day would not have been my first choice for riding a new horse up the mountain. But, I did it anyway because a lot of intangible but important things depended on it.

So there I was the next morning, *mecate* over my arm, bridle, bit, and reins wrapped around my waist walking up and onto the ice to bridle that jumpy, white-eyed, broom tail. Mr. Purdy's new horse was a scared beast, eyes more white than dark, his legs pumping hysterically, throwing off big clods of snow as he trotted frantically around the small enclosure to avoid my presence. I roped him as he tried, but failed, to sail over the fence, crashing dramatically back down onto the slippery ice onto his belly, his feet sprawled out—in which predicament I swiftly capitalized to get a halter over his ears, quickly and gently buckled him in—after which his whole sweating body was so tense and scared that he was as hard as an anvil.

A horse from a warmer climate no doubt, he didn't have enough fur on him for the cold, and the snow had him terrified. His mind was frozen too, but then I saw Bucky's soul pour into him like warm water as I sat on the poor downed horse's shaking back because when he finally rose I was mounted on a haltered horse, who didn't fight my presence. Leaning carefully over his left eye, I pulled the armpit-heated bit into his young mouth and the bridle up and over his ears, fastening the chin strap, experiencing the usual, bizarre stubbornness those damned little chin buckles always give a body just when you need them to buckle fast.

After dismounting, he tried to sidle off, but attached to me by the lead rope to the halter, he reared instead, slipped over backwards in the ice, and landed on his back.

Righting himself, he stood staring, a little stunned at his unexpected situation. I slipped the saddle blanket and saddle together up in one hopeful heave and very cleanly and slow, but in a moderately careless fashion, fastened the front and back cinches. He tried to crow hop as I tightened the front girth, but slid so violently on the ice that his feet started one after the other to basically run in place, until again he plopped down, all legs spraddled out, at which opportunity I climbed into the saddle while he was down and waited for him to stand.

I'd had the forethought of letting old Yella out into the fenced area down by the river, so once I opened the corral gate, I didn't have to worry about old Yella getting out on the asphalt and being hard to catch.

After I kicked off the top rung, effectively opening the "cowboy" gate of Conrad's jackleg corral, this horse's ears pricked up and away we went slipping, spraddling, and skating down the little hill in front, all the way to the creek, sliding backwards across the ice covered river, which to my immense surprise and relief held our weight, and spinning back forward we dug our way up the deep snow of the next hill, up onto the old tree-lined logging road that went for two miles diagonally up the forested mountainside. Icicles swayed and crashed everywhere, snow was falling, and this horse was sliding, spinning, then dropping down, but miraculously moving in a general trend up the steep, weird, ice-covered trail.

From every ponderosa, fir, juniper, and pine a wild screen of jangling icicles hung. And this horse was terrified of every icicle, so I named him Icicle.

He seemed pretty rusty and didn't respond much to turning at first, or stopping at all, for which result you had to turn him left then right and sort of slide into a stop sideways. I didn't even try to back on such ice and much less on a steep mountainside! But the real miracle was that he never totally rolled over backwards on top of me, or slipped down sideways to pin my leg, though he whomped his own kisser good enough to swell up the next day, after falling on his front legs a couple of times.

After a couple of miles of that, it was all prayers coming back down. So dangerously close to washing out in the ice did we come, that I gradually edged Icicle over into the deep, two foot snow of the surrounding forest to plow our way home. It was very cold and exhausting, but about half the way back down the two of us were pretty much a team: me steering and praying and him doing all the hard work.

When we got home to his little corral, unsaddling Icicle was harder than tacking him up. But once accomplished, I blanketed him till his sweat dried, then let him loose. He rolled cheerfully in the new powder snow, his eyes back in his sockets, and ate the hay I gave him like a teenager in a burger joint after a ballgame. Like a pro he just dipped his nose in the water bucket, knowing better than to drink while still hot, washed his teeth and ate snow instead.

Bucky had done it, though I don't think I really understood as well how much he'd done as I later would. The wife, I have to say, though amazed by the improbable outcome of such a wild adventure was not the least bit impressed with my ability to carry it off when such unnecessary risks brought us no food and was to her just a huge waste of time.

The next day Icicle was even harder to saddle and pretty

stiff from the previous day's scamper, but he loosened up half way to the top and to my delight actually started to throw his back into the work.

Everyday for three weeks we rode and when the snow began to thaw and mud was everywhere, I decided to steer him towards the more stable ground of the grassy zones along the creek. Just like the time before, Purdy took more than six weeks to reappear, rolling in when only the north sides of the hills had snow patches and the March pasque flowers had already poked out from under boulders, their furry coats still on. I hadn't minded though because I was riding the hell out of Icicle and more people came to be healed and our economics had started to perk up.

The two of us had been out riding when Conrad rolled in and seeing him from a cliff top we raced down to meet him. The mornings were still chilly, but deliciously full of sun shooting between the trees. The world was good, wet, and smelling of mud and spring, full of brightly colored birds as we rode up to Purdy's hay shed, where dismounting and unsaddling I noticed that Purdy had a look on the gray skin of his hungover face that made me glad I wasn't his son, an expression trying to hide a jaw dropped in surprise, while snarling with disgust and contempt.

"So, what happened anyway, how is it you're riding that horse?"

"You said I could ride 'em if I wanted to, remember? Well, I wanted to, so I did."

"Who trained him for you?"

"What do you mean?"

"That horse had never been touched by anyone; we had to drug him with a dart-gun just to trailer him; no one could ride him or even get within a mile of him; how is it you're out there riding him?"

"What are you talking about, Icicle here is a good horse, anybody, I mean anybody who can actually ride, could ride 'em I think. I wouldn't give 'em to your kid just yet, ride 'em yourself for another year, then I think Colter would be fine on him. I thought he was just sour and rusty because he hadn't been ridden for a while, but he's pretty good now and real strong on these hills. You should take him out and see for yourself."

Lighting a cigarette, Conrad Purdy slugged me in the gut and walking away to pull his briefcase out of the truck, his hat cocked back, and with a teeth-bearing grimace, without looking at me, yelled what was intended to be an insult, "Thanks a lot for breaking that bronc for me. I figured you'd be too stupid to see he was an outlaw and you'd break your neck trying to ride 'em." And then he walked off into his house.

He never paid what he owed on the hay and was no longer sympathetic with having me ride Icicle. For though the horse hated him and Purdy couldn't saddle him and none of his expert cronies could do any better, Purdy refused to ask the likes of me to help him with his horse.

Strangely, Conrad Purdy had felt attacked by the wildly rumorized account of my being able to ride Icicle when none of them could. Despite the fact he had twice set me up for failure and even destruction, when that destruction failed to happen, Purdy got it into his head that my capacity to ride Icicle was evidence of some highly trained expertise from a sophisticated former life which I was trying to hide from, in which I was guilty of some malfeasance and was on the lam, for which he too was now the unsuspecting victim, requiring an apology for making him look bad!

When the dust from that strange notion settled and nobody was buying it, then Purdy's superstitious, gambling, con-man instinct began to sense that something honestly powerful and mystical beyond his normal capacity to exploit, deceive, or fully comprehend surrounded us. Instead of gratitude and simple admiration for a job well done by people he had been casually victimizing, Purdy began to harbor a great fear of me, and kept away.

So, despite all my efforts to the contrary, once again I had no horse to ride, the Canyon Wren of spring had already commenced to sing, and we had been here for a year.

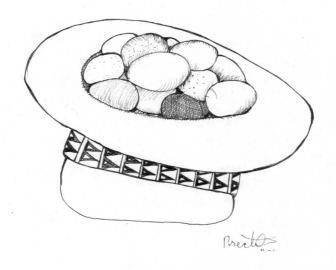

Chapter 7

Eggs

My mother's multinationed Indian father, like so many others of his vibrant descendancy, clamped himself into the American, single-culture lathe and watched painfully as he turned himself into a symmetrical spoke in a cog of the Big-Machine addicted world of the 1920's. Carving away as much of what appeared in him as Native as he could, shaving flat the spiritual integrity and noble-life-approach that his mother Louisa tried so hard to impart, whose presence might cause "white"-America-in-control to reject him for who he really was, my maternal grandfather decanted away his real ancestry until only a vague whiff of a very distant French gene remained to define the brew of who he told himself he had become, so the business world would gloss him for a legitimate, homogenized, pale citizen to gain admittance in the professional job market.

What little remained of him became a very talented, hard working but depressed, culturally-unconvinced automobile designer for Henry Ford in Detroit during the 1920's, 30's, and 40's, finally departing that limited existence by his own hand in the 1950's.

In our family mythology, he has been credited with being the major inspiration and initial designer of the original American pickup truck, in its earliest cute incarnation after World War 1.

For that reason, when I drove, I always owned Ford trucks, not because they were great, which for our family they were, but more out of a deep loyalty, not to the man he became, but to the Native he sacrificed to invent the pick-up truck with which we on the Reservation so thoroughly identified.

In those times, nobody had a car, only pickup trucks, so all the Indians I'd ever known felt, that of all American pickup trucks, Ford trucks had the best sound, which you must know had nothing to do with their engines, or transmissions, but with the sound their doors made when a couple of your friends thumped them with a sideways-fist while cruising down the long highway singing their hearts out. Ford doors all sound like big, grass-dance drums. In those days of my youth, we sang Indian songs accompanied by the deep boom of our truck doors everywhere we went. But even so, the differential and transmission, if you drove them with just the right touch, made such old Fords much more suited to the highly changeable temperatures and driving conditions, wet or dry, the rugged terrain, and the extreme use they were put to in New Mexico's diverse altitude, than any other.

That early spring, when the once frozen ground thawed by day, the untraversable sea of deep, red mud that was born from that extra-long winter's record snows gave my little, red, 1968 F150 a hero status and wide reputation.

Even as small children, all rural New Mexicans were taught that like it or not, springtime in a good wet year in the high desert plateau or mountain heights was a time when both driving and walking was always done only at night when the liquid ground froze hard as rock. For anyone disregarding this principle, even those boasting powerful, newer model, four wheel drive SUVs or trucks who'd been erroneously led to think that their vehicle was mysteriously equipped with something that made them immune to the laws of nature, who, compelled to get to the job as usual, or driven by ignorance, or with a bold irreverence for chance, chose to drive the unpaved "dirt" roads or even the short graveled entrances to their family, forest homes or sage-flat mansions, found themselves stalled out in muck, their differentials buried in the glue-like clay, their chassis floating on the mud like a dead cricket in a bowl of oatmeal, their wheels spinning aimlessly, spewing great rooster tails of mud in all directions.

It seemed as if people believed modernity was failing human progress if it couldn't provide constantly incrementing technology whose prime directive was to make it so nobody had to be outside of a vehicle or a building and that no skill should be necessary to live; that people, through machines, should be so powerful and capable that they could just carelessly plow ahead to *do* whatever they wanted, wherever they wanted, whenever they wanted, purposely ignoring the subtleties of the conditions Nature presented.

But when it came to New Mexico's springtime backroad mud and ice, a four wheel drive vehicle supplied with more power and independent wheel capacity, without the corresponding skill to drive one, generally just gave people more power to drill themselves even deeper and faster into the mud than anybody else in more humble conveyances. These fancy vehicles were often stuck in places where a simple rear wheel drive driven inventively by a driver accustomed to mud, slick hills, and narrow cattle guards, who drove always awake and suspicious of bad spots, and respectful of Nature's sense of humor might bring one safely down the same route without mishap. Otherwise, it was best to just stay home in April or drive at night.

Nonetheless, until the ground had dried and solidified a bit by May, my little Ford, with a long chain, pulled out truck after truck, car after car, both locals and visitors, to more solid ground, twice rescuing a peeved and thankless Conrad Purdy and even one of his cowboy friends in his jacked up, Arizona, four by four pickup, to boot.

Horses, especially teams of horses, were also very good at rescuing vehicles, cattle, or other horses stranded in springtime mud. It was from this skill, taught me by the same old Pueblo gentleman from whom I learned how to shoot a suffering horse, by which principle when extended to my old pick-up, together we were able to gently dislodge so many from winter snow banks and April's muddy grasp.

Faithfully cranking and starting up in every temperature, my old, rear wheel drive truck with its uncomplicated, straight-six engine steamed right along in every season and by the time Spring had gestated out of Mother Winter's stormy belly, the red Ford cheerfully conveyed us twice a month, west into Santa Fe, some thirty miles down and away from the mountains. Shopping and city business completed, she faithfully rolled us back to the animal and plant rich, creek-carved ravines where we camped.

By June the world looked, smelled, and sounded like a pagan paradise. The skies at dawn and dusk both glowed brilliant with abalone, the Canyon Wren sang, mama bears and babies eating ants and beetles, grazing grass, and digging out ground squirrels, snapped at bees, and hoped for honey; and while the Gods were dreaming of rain and I still without a horse, one morning, while driving a back road home alone, returning from a foray into town saw a timid sign that read *Home grown eggs / Everything for sale*. It had an arrow directing one to the left onto a rutted, dusty, dirt track that ran untenably straight up a hill at whose summit another sign pointed straight down the other side in a grade so steep the old truck had to take it in *granny gear*. The road bottomed out into a clearing, where cars parked randomly between the *sabina* juniper trees blanketing those hills left little space for me. A very fancy, very vertical, but very small "Santa Fe style" solar house of mostly glass was neatly installed on the side of the mountain that rose up immediately in front of the clearing.

To accommodate the intense slope, a steep stairway of wide lumber on heavy pylons switched back and forth up to the front door of the house over which people cradling lamps, a teapot, chairs, tatami mats, boxes of pots and pans, a bucket, a hoe, a shovel crawled down back to their cars.

One of them carrying a fat little hamster in a rectangular cage emerged from the house and trying to descend the stairway was effectively impeded by a red-cheeked, little girl with a lacy cotton dress and long blond hair who looked all the world like a Renoir painting, who between sobs complained bitterly in French to her very sympathetic young father, in a cashmere sweater and a short beard, who finally pulled her off of the man dragging away her pet.

Down where I'd parked, a well-made corral of milled poles and posts stood, to the rear of which, against the mountain, a very architectural loafing-shed presided, looking a lot like something from an old Russian fairy tale book.

Arguing over hay placed neatly in a real manger, two horses, one an oily, mouse-colored, black-pointed, grulla gelding, the other a small, well-built, toasted-sorrel mare with big soft eyes and a face-wide blaze that ran all the way over her nose and into her mouth, both squealed and kicked at each other raising a moderate cloud of dust.

Calling out to the little girl in French, a woman with a beautiful walk came forth from the corral shed clutching the handle of a legitimate French egg basket with some fifteen eggs of every color and size.

Expertly scaling the corral fence, she plopped down right next to me where I leaned, just as her distraught little girl ran up burying her face in her mother's dress pleading madly for her rodent who had already disappeared in a sedan struggling back up the hill.

Caressing her sad head, the mother spoke to me instead.

"Did you come to see the mare?"

"No, not really. Actually, I saw the sign for eggs."

"Well, here you are," she said a little too brusquely, trying to hide her own heartbreak. "The chickens were the first thing to get sold this morning. It's surreal that we still have their eggs."

Like the child, who had quieted a bit, she too looked teary and forlorn.

"Well Ma'am, these eggs are wonderful looking, I have to say."

All our chickens had frozen to death in the sub-zero winter. In Guatemala, where every family had their own birds, chickens who ate the same greens and food that the people lived on and laid a few precious, delicious eggs, "machine chicken" eggs, as the Tzutujil Maya called commercial farm produced eggs, tasted even worse in the States than they did in Central America. They were viewed by all highland Indians with enormous suspicion, the general theory being that they were some synthetic, egg-shaped, technological hoax and none of the Indians could be convinced these "eggs" were the product of a live animal. Native Mayans wouldn't eat them.

I bought a dozen of her eggs, putting them in my hat balanced on the truck seat, leaving this woman with her basket and three eggs. Though she offered them all, with the basket included, its never good to take the last of anything from people or Nature, not the last tortilla, or the last piece of bread, or the last piece of meat, or the last dollar, or the last berry on a bush, or the last fish in the sea, or to have to have the last word. It rubbed me the wrong way.

"If it's not too forward to ask, how come you are selling everything?"

As followers of some visionary, they had come with a group from France to make an intentional, "rural" community on the outskirts of the very-hip-culture of Santa Fe, New Mexico. They all bought land together to make a go at organic farming, run a vegetarian restaurant, and live together in a place with plenty of room.

But the winters had been too cold for most of them and when all their land partners fled to Hawaii, Bali, or Mexico, they stayed. The exhaustion and disappointment of such hard, back-breaking work in such a short growing season on the north shadow of a mountain in rocky ground had finally driven this last stalwart couple into the comfort of the arms of other lovers and hopes of a new geography as well.

They were dividing their lives, selling everything. Miréd and her daughter were returning to Europe, to the limestone canyons of Gourdon, France and Jacque was headed to northern California with his new companion.

The little girl was missing her hamster and her old life.

Naïve and defeated, the terrain had chewed them up and spit them out, all their idealistic hard work gone to nothing. They had

of course started out privileged, from lives with infinite choices
and didn't actually need to work, only doing so to obey a utopian
creed and to explore what the "experience" of real-life was like
on their route to "greater consciousness". With plenty of money
to buy their way into any adventure they dreamed up and plenty
of money to bail themselves out of any failures of their dreams, I,
who had none of that, nonetheless still felt so sad for all of them
losing their dream, their dishes, their chairs, their hamster, their
horses, the little girl losing the only life she'd ever known.

From where we stood that day with our backs leaning
against the corral rails, I could see out all the way over to the
Galisteo Basin and past, right to where my mother was buried
on the side of Sandia Mountain and right to where the rippling
flatter land dropped off to the Big River, where I grew up.

All three of us, the lady, the girl and I leaned there, quiet
now, all of us staring far away to what had been, to what might
happen, all with different histories and different reasons for
having grief as a constant companion, all of us wistful and
sad, but still daring to be hopeful.

Then, old Bucky made me talk:

"How much are you asking for your little mare?"

It didn't matter how much this horse might cost, I could
never buy her even if she was just a dollar, for I had no money to feed her, I had no corral, no hay, no pasture, no water
trough, no saddle, no bridle, no halter, no lead, no tarp for the
hay, hell, not even a simple rope, no nothing. The little money
I had was there to feed the family. How could my mouth talk
without asking me first?

"We had her for five hundred dollars, but I'll let you have her for four-fifty," she replied in a kind of musical way. I don't know why I said what I did, but I did say: "Would you take four hundred even?"

She yelled to Jacque, coming back down the stairs holding up a little table that a woman wanted him to strap on top of her Volvo. He yelled back, "Alright. That's good. Four hundred even. She's all yours; she's a wonderful horse; very gentle and good in the mountains."

"She's the only thing I'm really going to miss when we go back to France. Her name is Juniper," Miréd said in a very Frenchy sort of way.

For about five minutes we'd been hearing the gradual approach of a vehicle with its radio blaring over a hollow bang and boom echoing down the hill behind the lower-gear-growl of a bigger truck than mine, which eventually came into view, bouncing and clanking and finally landing into the flat of the clearing, from where it deftly backed a strange and massive, home-made-looking horse trailer of welded-steel plates within inches of where I stood, still pondering how I could buy Juniper with no money.

"Hey Martín, is that you?" croaked a voice from the cab, whose sound matched the character of its author. For when Dick, like an enthusiastic, amplified, pink raven who'd found a person suit, jumped out of the cab he was still hopping sideways when he hit the ground. Friendly, but always loud, "You're not stealing my horse out from under me are you?" he yelled.

"Hey Dick, how's it going? That's a pretty wild looking trailer you got there."

"You like it? It's still hot. I just finished welding it this morning! I thought I'd test it out on these people's crazy road and pick up this handsome fella. You know me, I love grullas. I've seen every grulla for sale within a hundred miles, this is the purdiest one so far."

A successful metal sculptor by expression, a rich man by birth, who owned a lot of 'blue sky land' south of Santa Fe, Dick loved horses and had inhaled a lot of toxic fumes. I barely knew him, but he always acted like we'd known each other for a century.

"Hey, I really enjoyed hearing how you put Conrad Purdy in his rightful place." And slapping me on the shoulder, "That was pretty good, you riding all that ice on his incorrigible bronc he thought would break your neck."

"I did no such thing. He said he was rideable, so I just got on him and rode. He turned out pretty good. I didn't even know he was rough stock, and I guess he forgot too."

"What are you doing here, looking at horses?"

"Yeah, I just bought that little mare right there." I couldn't believe I'd said that!

"That old thing? That's not much of a horse for you, now is she?"

"Nah, she'll come out real good, you just wait."

Then it happened again.

"Look Dick, I was wondering if you would be so inclined, if you had the time, to trailer this horse out to my place, 'cause I didn't bring a trailer."

"Oh yeah, I could do that, gimme a chance to test out this trailer on the highway."

I grew up in a town famous for the calm business resolve and audacity-made-friendly of its Native jewelery peddlers, some of which must have jumped into me as I shamelessly pushed my luck beyond all prudence.

"That would be a great help Dick, but if you're willing to do that, I was hoping you would lend me four hundred dollars so I can pay for this horse. I'll pay you back as soon as we get to the house, 'cause I came without my cash. I just came to buy eggs and then I saw this mare."

There was a little mountain silence until Dick, laughing like a hyena, pounded his truck hood until he choked. "Come on," he sputtered, "lets get loaded before you finagle anything else out of me."

The French couple were laughing too when Dick paid the nine hundred fifty for his gelding and the four hundred for my new mare in cash, but loading his new horse into this bizarre, rolling, sheet-metal closet turned out to be difficult. The little mare was ready to get going to her new life and got right in, but the grulla needed some magic to get him in. After watching Dick try all sorts of approaches to load this powerful gelding with no success, I remembered a can of sardines I had with my tortillas in the truck earmarked for my lunch.

I unrolled the lid of the little flat can and let the grulla sniff, then after placing it in the hay platform in the back of the trailer, we all ignored the horse, looked the other way, and in he went. Canned fish to the rescue again!

The eggs somehow survived the teeth-jarring climb up and away from there, riding cheerfully beside me in my hat as my old Ford followed Juniper's tail down the highway, east to Glorieta, hanging out of the back of Dick Laughy's home-made horse trailer.

I had a lot of trouble.

But,

I had eggs, that was good.

But,

I had no money and owed four hundred dollars now, that was bad.

But,

I had a horse, that was good.

But,

I had no corral, no halter, no rope, no hay, no water trough, no saddle, that was bad.

And,

I had no permission from the wife and family to go into debt for a horse they probably wouldn't want, that was the worst.

But,

I had eggs, that was good.

So on a spur, Bucky's soul made me do it. I revved up my truck and waving as I went by, passed Dick's rig on the road and headed home to get there before he did.

When I rounded the road where Purdy lived, I saw Colter, much bigger now, trying to ride old Yella.

Rushing home, I flew in with the eggs to everyone's delight, then reached into my wallbags and fished out old Bucky's braid of mane hair, hopped back in my truck and sped up and screeched to a halt at Purdy's, in a cloud of summer dust.

Jumping out of the cab just as Dick, motor running, pulled alongside to watch, I walked up to Colter, past Conrad on the rail, and handed him old Bucky's hair braid.

"Colt, I saved this for you last winter when I had to put your horse down. I put a silver holder on it so you can hang it how you want. I've been meaning to get it to you, but I haven't seen you until now."

It took the boy a minute to remember who I was and then he got down and shook my hand and thanked me for taking care of his pony and for bringing me his hair.

"Where I come from Colter, the hair of one horse gone is like a seed, it's supposed to cause a new horse to come. May it be so."

And as I turned to leave, Purdy grabbed my arm and slapped in my hand three hundred of the four hundred dollars he owed me for hay I bought to feed his horses last winter. I smiled; and he almost did too. Then, without asking, I leveled his debt by "borrowing" forty feet of soft cotton rope from his barn, along with four bales of hay, a galvanized bucket filled with pole barn nails, and after tossing the bales and the nails in the truck bed, with the rope coiled on one arm and the money still in my fist, I jumped back into the cab and took off just in time to catch up to Dick, who'd already started across the creek and up into our place.

When Dick saw I had no corral at all, I finally explained I'd gone for eggs and come back with a horse, and had just come up with only three hundred of what I owed him.

He laughed and banged his fist on the steering wheel and said the look on Conrad's face when he saw I had a horse of my own was worth at least a hundred dollars. He said with the three hundred, we were even.

Before unloading Juniper, I cut twelve feet of the cotton rope and quickly made a halter as taught to me by the same old timer who'd shown me how to kill quickly a suffering horse and how to pull tourists out of the mud. Fastening it over her sweet-smelling head, I led her out of the trailer, straight to a big ponderosa pine, and tied her there in its shade. I filled my new bucket full of water from the river, left it for her to drink, and cut open a bale and laid a slice on the ground, which she ate in her slow way.

Still grinning and fascinated, Dick asked:

"Where you thinking to keep her anyway?"

"Right where she is, in her corral" I replied.

"What corral is that?"

"The one I'm going to build around her right now."

Still laughing, Dick helped me lift the rails, as one by one I hammered the long, pole-barn nails through some old, crooked, dry aspen poles, using standing trees as posts, until I had a single-rail enclosure around where Juniper stood tied in the middle.

I'm probably the only guy to build a corral around a standing horse, instead of putting a horse into a standing corral!

Over the days I added more and more rails and when the corral had an entrance and I deemed it a corral, I released Juniper. People who'd been watching from the road just for the humor of the sight began cheering and honking their truck's horns.

Half Arabian and half Quarter Horse and at least fourteen years old, I could tell by the fact that the French couple had kept the hay up off the ground and inside a manger to keep out the sand and by the shape of her teeth, that Juniper had probably been a horse prone to colic. Old *Mesta* style horses only rarely sand-colicked, but "white man" horses brought from outside New Mexico often never acclimatized to all the windborne, microscopic dust and sand in everything, especially in the wild grass and in all the local hay and most ended up with a belly-ache caused by a sediment of clay and intestinal juices, or worse yet, big balls of indurated clay and sand accumulated over time that obstructed digestion so thoroughly, if it led to bloat, the pressure could kill a horse fairly quickly, if no relief was found. Also, because of the constant presence of sand in their New Mexico diet, modern horses' soft teeth ground into strange shapes quicker too, causing them to chew inadequately, and forced to swallow large fibers, the gut could often "tie up" with undigested fiber obstructions as well, causing a dangerous colic.

Most local horses of the *Mesta* type had a different schedule of teeth eruption and a much denser bone and enamel structure, partly because generationally such horses, even in Spain five hundred years before, were used to getting their necessary salt and minerals from the dissolved minerals in churned up water. Modern people don't watch the wild enough to know that horses, some deer, all buffalos, elk, antelope, and moose, who all prefer good wild water, but make that natural, clear water murky with mud before they drink, which is why so many horses have the inborn tradition to muddy the edge of a pond by striking it with their front hooves, or even rile up the water in their water troughs, in an attempt to purposefully ingest the same dust and sand of dissolved mineral salts and silica that in more civilized animals cause their guts to seize up, but give life to the more natural horse.

Also, horses whose feet had never had to consistently climb hard rock, run hard over gravely ground, or negotiate deep sand often developed hoof walls that thinned out over time, then dried, or even rotted, then cracked and dislaminated, sand grains often wedging the cracks open.

A horse's hoof was like a tooth that digested and absorbed the world he ran joyfully across, all the running and pounding, with no weight on their backs, caused good peristalsis in the gut and a tremendous circulation that made a strong mind and bone.

When confined to soft turfy pastures, plastic water troughs with non-mineral water and pre-pulverized-by-product soft feeds horses' bodies and minds, like people, begin to atrophy and begin to genetically give birth to overly delicate horses with already special, human-dependent existences at birth. Ironically, such horses are easily destroyed by the very things in nature that actually give life and increased vitality to a natural horse.

Juniper was easy going, but not so strong, and had trouble on the steeper hills, her breathing was noisy and troubled, her hoof walls weak. So I forced her to move as much as I could, to gradually strengthen her. But considering I was riding her without saddle or bridle, mostly because I didn't own either, we couldn't really go the necessary distance to get her in shape.

A well fitting saddle, with stirrups, helps distribute a good rider's weight and equilibrium more evenly over a horse's physique, especially in steep, up-and-down terrain. Whereas riding bareback, no matter how skinny, light, and balanced a rider might be, transfers all the rider's weight and movement from the hip bones right to two small spots on either side of the horse's spine, impairing the nerve flow up and down the back and often causes the rider to hang on a bit with her legs, causing difficulty with the horse's rib fascia and can so easily confuse leg signals.

But, be that as it may, a saddle had I none, so bareback it was.

Moving through the wild highland cliffs, trees, and animals of summer pumped my soul's blood back into a long deprived crevice in myself, where what I really might be hibernated, hopeful and formulating like an insect in a chrysalis. As we rode, I rode toward myself a little more each day.

In a way she'd probably never been, I wanted Juniper to get strong, though with horses its hard to judge, for if even once in their earlier life they have gone all the way into being in some kind of shape, then no matter whatever transpires, even years of being forgotten in some pen, if you look hard, you can generally see a layer of fire and capacity still rippling through their fascia. And that's what I saw.

The little mare had done something, somewhere, for someone. But to really get going I needed a saddle, so, of course having no money and remembering all my mother's and father's resourceful ancestors and all the intensely clever inventive Native spirit I'd grown up with, where people created all sorts of inventions with what was available to solve every situation in farming, in the kitchen, as kids with home grown toys, I decided to make myself and Juniper a saddle!

Old saddles were everywhere when I was growing up, pack saddles, old cowboy saddles with high cantles, narrow swells, and wooden trees, but none of them had been held together like modern saddles with screws or glue, nails or staples, but expertly sewn and tied with rawhide, that much forgotten incredible material.

I burned holes in pieces of elk antler sheds that I'd cut into two big Y's and after splitting two, identical, slightly-curved boards out of a cottonwood stump, I carved those into saddle bars and burned holes to correspond to my antler "pommel" and my antler "cantle" and with wet elk rawhide cords I tied the frame together.

A friendly, young man who always visited our camp returning from trout fishing up the Pecos drainage, who'd brought us the first recordings of Mongolian throat singing, the first South African Township accordion music I ever heard, and the first released pictures of the frozen horses and other funeral offerings from ancient Altaic horse nomad tombs housed in the Hermitage, when he heard about the horse, came over and started yelling in disbelief:

"Martín you're crazy, do you actually think you can just make a saddle? With no shop, no real tools, with a pocket knife, a pliers, and a claw hammer? Saddles are complicated and difficult and take years to learn how to make. You can't just make a saddle!"

"Maybe yes, maybe no, but the old-time Natives, they made their own saddles with just the same antlers, wood, and rawhide and strapped 'em on their ponies and away they went and nobody could catch them. I think I can make a saddle."

And I did.

It was very minimal, sculptural in a way, and it had a good homemade cinch, a slim breast collar with homemade wood and rawhide stirrups.

It took two weeks to fully dry the rawhide I'd stretched over the whole affair and it was hard to wait. When it was dry, I eased it over an old sheep skin and let Juniper sniff it and after she approved it, I slipped it onto her sweet, red back. She didn't balk when I strapped this contraption on her and after tossing a wool blanket over the seat, I mounted. It was light, not exactly comfy, but it didn't dig into her back and using a halter as a bridle, like a dragonfly riding an eagle, away we flew.

There was no trail we did not dust and no height of mountain we did not try; I was going again; the Canyon Wren was singing. I had a horse!

But I didn't have a bridle. So, of course, I half-softened some more of the elk skin, painted it with old-time designs using black walnut and red earth and made a beautiful headstall that I still have now, thirty-five years later. At the bottom of the pail Purdey's nails came in, a rusty, old, wagon-horse snaffle bit had been tossed. I fastened this onto the bridle, attached cotton ropes for the reins, and we were off and going, Juniper turning brilliantly, one-handed on the neck in a way I hadn't even suspected.

Now I worked her hard over the ridges and Juniper was daily getting stronger, I fed her on the mountain grass and on the riverside oaks and willows, but then one day she began to bleed from her nose.

Where I grew up the old people said this was caused by the jealous thoughts of hidden detractors and could be countered by cutting off and powdering some of the ergots of the afflicted horse and burning them and having her inhale the smoke, then ridden hard to a sweat and given spruce needle tea instead of water.

She got wild and antsy after that treatment, but the bleeding went away, and soon she was running up the hills like a wild mountain sheep. Everywhere we went we only ran, never once tripping, or stumbling, or balking in any form. She got powerful and head-strong and friendly in a war-buddy kind of way.

We tore through streams and up mountain sides, snuck under water falls and sometimes just sat on a mesa-top in the sunlight, digging the grandeur of the mountains still snow-capped in July and the forested, high-land canyons that radiated out for miles in every direction filled with an opaque haze of blue light.

I'd gone for eggs and with no money came home with a pony. She was my horse; she sweated hard and we were happy. Must have been Bucky's last move for us because the

Pleiades, leader of the Dawn Star Horses of the Sun, were now on the horizon every morning and he must've finally run to join the Sun's herd. But he left me Juniper, a chicken-snare-saddle, a reputation, and my soul.

Chapter 8

Mouse

Sometimes we cantered the whole distance. Other times we trotted hard halfway, then walked and jumped up the sandstone terraced planks the remainder. At other rare times we did it all at dawn in the purple dimness, feeling our way up totally by faith, risking the crumbly knife edge ridges at nine thousand feet. But, however we went, when Juniper and I had climbed up the last rise to the very pinnacle of this forested mountain, locally known as The Cross, we came up on it from the east, where I had to dismount to proceed in single file over a precariously narrow razor edge onto a tiny spot that opened right in front of an ancient Pueblo world shrine. This beautiful place was the very, very, tip-top of the mountain.

The central granite shaft of this old-time, holy place had an ornate, curly, 17th century, cruciform, Spanish livestock brand deeply carved into its matrix to mark the corner of an old private Spanish land grant, which American mapmakers two hundred years later mistook for a Spanish Christian cross. Though the tiny, cobbled clearing before this elegant, high altitude shrine was too small to even dream of turning a horse around without careening to one's demise, eight hundred feet below, and barely big enough for a person to kneel, it was plenty big enough to host a troop of a thousand dancing Rain Gods. For it was here that Cloud Beings from more northerly mountains would swoop down to retrieve their "food": the offerings Natives left there, to fuel their journey south in their campaign against summer dryness in the lowlands. From this tiny spot the immensity of the inner spirits of the inner forms of all the entire world could be communicated with, and Indigenous Rain Gods summoned. The breath-taking vista from there ran by sight all the way from Sandia Peak to Mount Taylor, to Chicoma, to Lake Peak, past Mineral Hill out to the eastern plains and beyond, at least three thousand square miles all around! This vista was considered the nervous system of the Holy World, upon whose line of sight the Rain Gods could travel as quick as thought through the body of the Earth from sacred peak to sacred peak. Their seeing was their coming and going. They traveled on the light.

Almost twice a week, for most of the year, Juniper and I steered our way up to The Cross, following the faint remainder of an overgrown trail that in the beginning of our rides could hardly be made out by either of us.

These trails had been anciently worn into the mountain's rocks, roots, and earth by mountain sheep, when those animals were still the aristocracy of these high peaks and ridges. Though the sheep were all gone now, we could still follow their trails, for they were trails made by and for quadrupeds and kept expertly to all the higher ridges, emerging cleanly and cleverly from between the giant trees, in a route worked out by wild sheep long ago, that ran right between seemingly impassable stupendous chunks of vertical stone. This trail, little by little, re-emerged over the months from our constant passing and the pounding of Juniper's hooves, to the point where most of it was once again clear enough to follow.

It was not the only way to get to the top with a horse, but the only way from our side of the mountain. It seemed to be our secret path, for no others seemed to have discovered it. Probably because the trail had been so fabulously surveyed by the minds of such agile animals ages before, it required some fairly serious, vertical jumping from stone ledge to stone ledge, on cliffs that left only a conjectural trail, but whose passage, though clear to me, was so hair raising, that until both Juniper and I had attained our present adroitness and physical stamina together, I had not been willing to attempt.

On the opposite side of the mountain, though the approach was even steeper, a famous cave was hidden there, from whose entrance the summit could be reached fairly easily on foot. This cave had been the home of an ancient Pueblo ritual society, whose priests for centuries had served this mountain regularly, depositing traditional offerings at the shrine on the peak to feed the life-giving Gods of the Wild that came there to feast. Though the wild sheep had been extirpated and their people rudely driven from the area one hundred and fifty years before, the spirits they served live there still, pushing life in from their mountain. Natives throughout the state still maintain an old ritual obligation to the place, albeit, at a distance, and very secretly.

To climb the peak was never a goal for me, but rather a holy place where we added our own offering and our prayers for the world to receive. It was not for the challenge or the exhilaration of climbing a mountain on horseback for which we climbed, but as a means to approach a sacred depot where Gods, unhindered by the aimless noise and withering scrutiny of modern people, could still be approached! Our riding was part of the prayer we made.

So now, in a modicum of good physical shape, the two of us routinely made the cliff crossing to The Cross in an adrenalin rush of satisfaction that made our prayer and the offerings we left for the Holies at the peak all the more precious: because it took effort, danger, and dedication to deliver our gifts, from us to a time beyond our own. Love and true beauty always involve hard work, vision, a certain negotiation of difficulty, and not a small reserve of natural instinct.

The irony was that the mountain sheep trail had been made only for going up the mountain, not for coming down, because, of course for the mountain sheep, the climb up to this peak was not their goal either, neither was it just another routine ripple in the vastness of their territory. They came here to

The Cross as a means to gain access to a rich mineral lick that lay on the steep side of the next razor ridge, below and beyond The Cross, where no being without wings, much less a human on foot, could have lowered into without ropes and pitons.

This meant that together Juniper and I could never have survived if we'd tried to return by the same route we had come up on. We were pretty good on these cliffs, but we weren't mountain sheep. While it had been possible to jump up at certain angles onto some of the higher, terraced, rock ledges, to jump down some of those same ledges was impossible. You could not discern anywhere to land on the descent because the same overhangs blocked the view, and if you missed five hundred foot drops awaited. It was too steep and dangerous.

So after praying at the shrine on top of The Cross, Juniper and I had to back up, crossing in reverse the same one hundred foot of razor edge we'd come in on. Then carefully turning Juniper around to the left, and remounting, we dropped down the southern face by a different descending route of my own invention. Though we achieved it mounted, it too was precariously steep and mined out in the middle with a belt of an almost impassable, thick tangle of scrub oaks and raspberry bushes, after which we had to painstakingly pick our way over a large zone of sliding, unstable, granite slabs and scree—through which I steered, but Juniper, with her better eyes, strong joints, and expert judgment, always brought us to safely land down onto the more solid, flattish ground at the base of the mountain—next to our beloved creek, only a mile and a half upstream from our home. Unfortunately, by this route, we had to enter about two hundred yards inside the unmarked back boundary of land officially claimed by an intimidating and strangely out of place fortress-like protestant Christian retreat center, whose church spire bristled up like a rocket out of the forest a half mile away.

If we were careful not to be seen by these "Christians" where we landed, who didn't like any locals traveling over "their" territory, we could easily renavigate, quietly and invisibly, another old trail running forgotten along the base of the mountain, that led straight home through the big conifers, in one third the time and distance it would have taken us to return by our ascending route, if that had even been a possibility.

They never once saw us moving through the backstage of their theatre of operation, where out in "front", at the automobile entrance, a barricade with a guardhouse presided, from which armed security people in blue uniforms checked documents like a military base. "Our type" were always denied passage and turned back.

After all the exhilaration of such grand mountain riding, praying to the Gods I loved, and the soul healing reaffirmation that I could still out-maneuver some of the myopic opponents of my lifestyle who hated my reverence of the land as deity— knowing that we could still give the Empire the slip moving invisibly on horseback, merging like wind into the surrounding forest and terrain—there was still one very tiny section of our twice weekly pilgrimage for which I was unable to gain passage.

Less than a hundred yards upstream from the land where we camped, a little stone-lined wash, not two feet wide and only one foot deep, ran across this very convenient trail between the base of the big mountain and the creek. After jumping one thousand foot deep ravines and darting down whole mountainsides of stone, one would not even have noticed it as a feature if it had not been for the fact that whenever Juniper and I, within spitting distance of a good meal and home, came to the edge of this otherwise barely noticeable stone ditch, Juniper wouldn't budge and refused to pass over it into our camp!

Planting her otherwise reasonable feet, she would not be urged, pushed, talked into, waited for, or towed by rope, swatted from behind, spurred, coaxed, scolded into, cajoled, baited by grain or fish, nothing could make her move forward across this tiny wash.

I was forced to obey this one inexplicable and surprising quirk, for then to get home, she would only accept a detour of almost an entire mile, around to the south, all the way to the asphalt and onto the grassy easement of the highway, that for about one hundred and fifty feet ran right smack in front of Conrad Purdy's tourist trap, until we could merge back into the woods, cross our beloved stream, and ride up into our place.

This was not, strictly speaking, a real problem, just a minor irritation. It was, however, an enormous mystery: for horses love going home and Juniper from any other approach rolled right on in with no qualms.

She had made herself famous for crossing streams and rivers, didn't even balk on a swinging bridge. She had taken me on railroad tracks or alongside railroad tracks with blaring freight trains blasting by, she was steady along highways with or without auto traffic, steady around gunfire, lightening, loud radios, and wailing chainsaws; yet when we rode up to this quiet, tiny, flower-filled gully, under the ponderosas, practically right next to her own corral, she broke out in a cold sweat, her eyes bugged-out and going stiff, would back up and bolt away in the only instance of sheer hysterical terror she ever evidenced since I'd gone out for eggs and come home with her.

What was it about this pretty, stone trough that drained winter snowmelt in the spring, that was full of short, white asters all summer and pasque flowers bursting through in the spring snow, that every time we came close, Juniper panicked and would not cross?

The first time it happened, after getting home by alternate route, I returned later to the place alone on foot. I searched high and low, out and around, sniffed and listened, sat down and waited. One could hear our dogs barking and people laughing from the camp and even clearly see the flat roof of our cabin, the poles of the tipis peeking above the trees and the dirt track that ran through the creek! The world was even rather cozy here, nothing smelled dangerous, or sounded odd, or looked menacing, that I could tell, but then horses can see, hear, and smell the meaning in a lot of stratas of reality most people barely notice.

People tend to consider their horse as if he or she were some kind of inanimate object. Like a motorized canoe into whose seat they plop, expecting to be faithfully hauled wherever they direct, using the reins like a tiller, moving along the road to a given destination as if it were a river. For me, on the other hand, I always felt that most of the horses I loved riding were themselves the river, and it was my person who was the kayak being carried by the river's own flow. With my soul as the rider, my body could understand that the horse was a river with whom I moved, carrying us along the earth, rising and lowering, bending, curving, and straightening, even jumping the banks when she needed, and like a river, constantly and instantly adjusting to whatever conditions the wide earth demanded. It was as if a real horse was always flowing, like a peaceful, slow-moving creek, even when just standing unridden or asleep in a corral; where the act of saddling up was the putting of my kayak into the water.

Riding in this fashion makes it so our souls, as riders, must cruise only by always pushing ahead in concordance with the force and mind of the river; kayaking through and not harnessing its force. This means that one always *pushes* a horse into a turn and *pushes* into a stop, for horses — even trying to stand still — are actually still moving, like a slow moving river, constantly heading home to the sea, to the herd, to home.

But sometimes there's an unnatural spirit dam, some spirit obstacle people have unwittingly created but fail to see, something that blocks the "river's" flow, something that forces a horse's spirit, like water, to divert elsewhere. When this happens, a horse refuses to go where we want and must go another route, just like Juniper. For a lot of horse people, the very idea of not being obeyed means they are not in control and this scares people. These kinds of people usually spend a lot of their lives trying every new popular training fad to get their horse to do their rider's will. Trainers make every effort to ensure that a horse is as predictable as a machine. That is what they call a dependable and well trained horse.

Having ridden only half-broke, but very vital, reservation Indian ponies in my youth, I never really knew what amazing obedience civilized nations had hammered into their horses, in which all sorts of subtle cues and commands had horses mechanically yielding to the left, right, up, down, back, over, under, around, and through, head down, neck arched, always on the correct lead, etc.: all hand-me-down war-horse moves. We had none of that. For us, a dependable horse meant a horse that got us home safe off a trailless mountain in a blizzard, despite the fact that what we might be cueing our horse to execute would have killed us both in a flash at the bottom of a ravine or left us frozen to death with broken legs under a rock slide: the horse overriding our will and bad decisions in order to save us all.

That was a dependable horse.

We didn't want to ride horses so blindly and mechanical- ly obedient that they would loyally take us over a cliff if we asked them to do so. We wanted horses that were loyal to life and to their rider's will only when that was one and the same. Modern people say a horse that knows danger and shies away from it has a strong instinct and people will spend hundreds of hours "desensitizing" a horse's so-called instinct to get him to mechanically perform the moves people demand, without questioning.

But, like Juniper forcing another route on us around the little draw, there had to be more to a horse's refusal to do something than primal instinct. When a horse's river-flow hits a spiritual dam and they want to go around, that dam is made of some history encoded in the ground or air that your horse can clearly see, and you cannot, and is trying to save both of your lives by refusing to go over the edge.

The thing one must remember is the fact that horses can *see* the layers of what has happened in a place. They can and do literally *see* and *smell* history; not just human history, but all the simultaneous layers of what has happened in every inch of the ground on which they stand or traverse.

All these layers of animal, people, plant, and geological history are things horses experience as a vivid composite personality of what happened in a place. That "personality" confronts them as they try to pass, which can be Angelic or Ogreish or both. Horses that have "been around" know what to spook at and what's just a normal million years of history!

Horses see history in wholeness; like a river must sense the immense layers of ancient silt made before, combined with the layer the river itself lays down today.

When these layers of reality are cut through and exposed by water or by humans altering and ripping the ground, the water, and the air, a slice of the story of everything that ever happened in that place is released in a kind of pheromonal cocktail of non-sequential time, whose composite meaning assaults the spiritual senses of your horse as a single giant event, and takes over the horse, making him part of the story. When this happens, horses temporarily *become* the memory of what happened in that place: good, bad, amazing, ugly, or incomprehensible and often begin acting out what happened. For them, the physical world is a reservoir of memories, still alive and living in layers of what happened in a place, alongside with what is happening now, forming the very landscape of the world over which they, like a river, flow.

But...

On some trails the history is not actually so awful, but such that your horse, like a river, refuses to flow out of the courtesy and awe due to some grand happening of the past. Unknown to the rider, some ancient moment whose presence is very beautiful and special is spiritually fossilized into the land and totally apparent to certain horses—such land becomes sacred. Dependable horses do not lightly travel over what is truly Holy ground to them. People would do well to follow suit.

Some people say that horses can see ghosts. While dogs do see ghosts, horses actually see whole past situations, both magnificent and horrible, where all the layers of past situations encode themselves in the landscape. Horses not only read each other's breath, they also read the breath of the Earth's history as they move over Her. That is why sometimes they do unexpected, peculiar, out-of-character things when crossing certain areas: what to their rider seems for no apparent reason.

If you and your horse come to a spot where the history is bad and remains like a devouring hole, still hungry with human vengeance and looking for more, then your pony, if not desensitized, will smell the danger and insist that you navigate to another safer route.

When you are your horse's herd, this capacity that horses have to snort and warn you of danger, even one you can't see or that hasn't happened yet, and carry you to safety is what ancient horse cultures world-wide mean when their folktales say that horses can speak to people. You just have to understand that horses speak in actions.

In Juniper's case, I had no need for her to cross that tiny stone wash, for no doubt some ancient fumes of either something grand or maybe dangerous rose there from the history written in the rock causing her to deflect her flow according to her horse tribe's spiritual law. In the end it was her own business anyway and our detour soon became a regular tradition, as silly as it seemed to some.

By then the summertime heat in the mountains, though always cooler than the sea-like, wide stretches of high-desert that shimmered lower down, usually hit a stage when the air sat heavy and intoxicating with the mysterious, half-rank, half-sweet, powdery, aromatic recipe of wild flowers and mountain cactus seeking bees—trying to cut through the smell of pine needles, fir, piñon, and mountain juniper leaf oils caramelizing in the sun—while the more sensible perfume of lichens and the smell of hot stones buoyed up the general lusty rankness of the little creek's beaver mud, hissing rushes, and cattails.

Breathing such an atmosphere, no person or animal could even think straight for weeks: the whole world was delicious and became a young, ample mother who suckled a person's mind into a lovely infant-like stupor—making it almost impossible not to doze and dream—her lullaby of bees, bark beetles, cicadas, bird song, and flies finishing the job.

These hot, wonderful days were upon us all. Even evil-minded people found it too much effort to concoct maliciousness and our own spirits swam through the honey of each day in slow motion, eye lids half-lifted, almost dreaming, while almost awake.

And in one of these afternoons, Juniper and myself, her drowsy rider, returning from our jaunt up to The Cross, while taking that last little stretch of flat-end-trail at a walk along the creek, both began to uncontrollably drift off. Bouncing back almost awake by the occasional jolt of Juniper's lazy gait along the creek, both of our heads sweetly dazed and bobbling, both of us so much on automatic-pilot and so deliciously half-asleep and so smiling-silly-drunk upon the *delicia* of those once-a-year smells, that when we came to the cut-off to our now very accustomed detour, around and away from the dreaded draw, both of us failed to make the turn or even notice we'd passed it. Persisting on the trail, Juniper, her ears straight forward, realizing it too late, brought us to such a rude, jerking stop that I, in my very relaxed sleepy state, dropped effortlessly out of the saddle, landing right on my bottom, comically seated right next to the unpassable ditch!

While righting the reins, and myself more awake now, I

heard a little sound. Juniper, instead of pulling to bolt, was listening too; her ears moving in tandem to follow the whereabouts of the tiny little sound.

Both of us listened hard; and there it was.

The stones in the draw were singing! And a pretty little sound it was; but from under the rocks it came, a strange, mostly high-pitched, percolating, warbling tune.

Then it stopped.

The Canyon Wren was singing too, way up in the canyons, slow and faint and a little off key, just as drunk on summer as all the rest.

The draw began to sing again.

Still seated on the ground, I watched my horse and stared exactly where she stared and listened where she listened, and kneeling, I closed in onto where Juniper was peering bug-eyed.

The rocks warbled again.

The song was almost bird-like, but then it wasn't. It was chirpier, but with a long bent-note *coloratura* at the end of its ever-changing phrases, like what some minuscule singer of old Italian operas would do, but in a very, very high pitch.

Then it was gone.

Then it was back.

Where was it coming from, from the rocks themselves?

Medicine men had rocks that tinkled and spoke in their bundles. I had some myself, but this was different.

Then, there it came again.

Juniper, for some reason, her courage bolstered, very quietly came up a little closer and putting her head down by mine where I knelt, started snuffling and breathing in the smell of the sound from right where the tiny, beautiful, churning, little vibrato was coming from and then...

We saw him!

Juniper, her eyes even more bugged out, ears stiff and forward, all of her tensed and ready to explode, nonetheless inched her nose forward, nostrils flared, and I began to smile.

My horse and I were being serenaded by an extraordinarily unafraid and very capable singing mouse! Two and a half inches tall, sitting up on his hind legs, his tail wrapped around him, each front paw holding the other, his mouth held round and undulating — looking every bit like a tiny, funny Pavarotti — this wild, mountain mouse was unabashedly singing aria after aria, no two the same.

I tried so very hard not to laugh.

Then I tried even harder, but finally I had to, and I could not stop.

Juniper tried to make a break for it, but I held her lead tight while I laughed uncontrollably, quaking and rolling on the ground for at least a half an hour, the mouse singing the whole time though, as if singing right to Juniper. I'd been such an idiot not to have seen this singing mouse, who for months must have thought that Juniper was the biggest, most beautiful, golden-red mouse he'd ever seen and was scaring her with his shrill, high-frequency love tunes! It was all so great and hopeful and wild and natural. The laughing and crying just kept bubbling up out of me like a spring flowing into the river of our ride. We'd all heard about singing mice, but I'd never actually heard one singing.

I'm sure he was courting her because, after that, whenever we came to his arroyo he would come out and scare her with his song. She really was kind of like a giant, beautiful mouse. Then, I always had to laugh some more.

And ever after that, this event no doubt was deified into the matrix of the place and became a beautiful spiritual fossil in a layer very few humans would ever see and one to which all beasts would listen and respectfully go around—for in the end it actually was the rock whose heart was really singing through a mouse in love with a horse, whose body is the river, that the gully wanted to embrace, running through him every spring. For no matter how many times in the summer we stood and listened to his ever increasing repertoire and expert singing, Juniper, out of respect, would get scared, never cross the little wash and always try to run and we still had to take the detour to get home.

But if a horse is a river, what else should rivers do but run when the rocks that would hold them sing them into life?

Chapter 9
Shindai

Rolling down the old road to the plaza, just before entering the actual town of Santa Fe, we slowed up to survey the row of parked trucks of roadside vendors. Here for sale, you could find everything: firewood, flagstone, vigas, fence posts, sweetcorn, squash-vine tips, green chile, herbal medicine, barks, leaves, flowers, roots, and patent remedies, osha, piñon nuts, rugs, blankets, prepared food, and potted plants. I pulled off the road and up to a dapper, old-style *viejito* tying hanks of oat straw into little toy donkeys, stars, and chickens sitting between his old, blue, Chevy Apache truck bed filled with those very good, small, old-time, red New Mexico apples and four very neat, small, old-style bales of crunchy, sweet-smelling, orchard grass hay.

We got along right away because, speaking in New Mexico Spanish, I bet him that his tractor was an old blue Ford and that his baler was a red one, the kind that made such small but perfect twine tied bales light enough for even a ten-year-old to lift, and when I guessed correctly that the apples, the oats, and the hay all came from Alcalde, some forty miles north, he gave me two bushels of apples for the family, without charge, and said if we came to his house on the morrow we could keep for free as much fruit as we could pick in a day.

I was looking for hay for Juniper. When asked about the bales, that well-dressed old man said he had forty more at his farm and if I would take them all he would drive them to my house in Glorieta for three dollars and fifty cents a piece. If we came the following day to his place to clean up his orchard of all these late-summer apples, he would follow our truck back to our place loaded with hay.

We had a place now where to shelter such a prize, for a carpenter whose wife had been helped a bit by my Native medicine approach to healing a situation with her womb, had paid me by building a small but very useful hay shed on the side of the hill just up and behind Juniper's comically natural, meandering, hillside corral.

With his expensive Italian fedora, black and full of sterling silver pins—cocked back on his head—a starched, white, long-sleeve shirt, ironed black slacks held up with a black belt with tiny sterling conchos and a turquoise studded buckle, his lace-up work boots shined, a black vest and a small silver bolo tie that matched the buckle, Don Ramón, the next day, true to his word and more, helped us fill up our truck bed with the best late-summer apples and faithfully drove his blue Apache behind my red Ford the seventy-some miles into the mountains, helping me unload the bales into the shed.

New Mexico still had a little whiff of its old goodness in those days, and while the whole family, in the company of Ramón's very friendly wife Doña Cata, sat bathing in the laughter and taking in *la platica*, we sat in the shade of a cottonwood, drank coffee and shared some sweet-bread she had brought along. Don Ramón, realizing early on that the little bales were probably for Juniper and would take her only four months to finish eating, told me that his granddaughter living on the Santa Cruz River just east of Española had another forty bales of very similar hay that he thought I could buy for two dollars each if I wanted them.

We were making some good cash now and though, at that price, such a deal sounded too good to be true, I chased it down anyway hoping for once to have enough feed to last the winter without having to pay off-season prices.

The next day, after bouncing down the bluff onto the riverside bosque flat where Ramón's young granddaughter and scared husband had their little place, there in a very small pen made of old bedsprings, car doors, and sundry flat objects called into service as fencing material, each wired onto the next, stood a powerfully-built, little gelding of a color we used to call a dirty paint with wild, blue-and-black eyes ringed with white, a thick black mane that almost reached his knees, and a tail that matched.

At that price, the hay of course had disappeared long before I could even get there, but Ramón's beautiful grand-daughter Letti, with her baby on her hip, didn't waste any time letting me know that her husband, a young guy in a small felt cowboy hat, with scared, flitty eyes was selling the horse for one hundred and fifty dollars, which included his saddle. They needed the cash.

The horse was both homely and magnificent at the same time and looked like he was probably scheming, always a bad sign.

"He's trained to do tricks in the parade."

This little paint who they called Wiener lived in quarters so tight he could barely turn around, which no doubt account-ed for his snorty, pent-up demeanor, constantly arched neck, and that look in his eye like he was waiting to execute a secret plan, none of which would have comforted a prospective buy-er's foreboding.

"He's trained to ride in parades, he can stand up and walk on two legs just like a person, he loves it, he can dance around in circles on two legs, you want me to show you?"

The little paint was full of dodges and when JoJo climbed into the pen, the horse did everything you don't really want a horse to do, except he didn't bite or kick. But he did balk, avoided the halter, and once haltered, tried to rear; but JoJo, without one break, continued his stream of praise for the horse, and never batting an eyelash as he dodged and pulled the horse around and out to a tying post, threw a pretty good saddle up onto this heavy-withered, wound-up pony—who skittered and side-stepped throughout—but who, once buckled in, stopped rearing and stood stock still, looking as if he was gathering steam to explode any minute. But, he never did.

Wiener had wound himself around and around until he had snubbed himself solidly to the massive post, while JoJo still talking, ran into and out of the garage returning with an awful looking, home-made piece of hardware with which he intended to "bridle" this "trained" horse. I'd seen some bad gizmos people had designed to ride so-called problem horses with but this one was built by a very imaginative fiend. This top heavy rig sported a curved-nose-band made of bent rebar with long shanks, like levers, attached to a kind of sliding, gag-bar bit, a bicycle-chain curb strap, and rope reins knotted onto these shanks with smaller diameter chains, all very casually and unconvincingly tied onto a flimsy headstall made of braided hay twine. Surprisingly, this insane apparatus was very easily slipped into the horses mouth and over his velvety, snorting, dirty paint nostrils, pulled over one ear, then the next, and with no throat latch, deemed to be in place.

Unclipping the halter-lead JoJo, with great agility, was in the saddle, spurring Wiener around in tight circles, still talking with no punctuation.

"Watch, watch," JoJo blurted, loud enough to scare all the horses in the next county, "watch, watch how he dances," and with that he backed his beast up and then stopping, gave the reins a sharp tug and up rose Wiener onto his strong hind legs, his forelegs dangling, like a corgi dog begging for a biscuit, after which the horse started sidestepping to the left in a tight little circle until he'd done three hundred and sixty degrees.

JoJo tapped his neck and Wiener dropped to all fours, and prancing slowly in place, looked like he was ready to go... somewhere.

I'd come for hay but now I was looking at a horse that could beg for a biscuit. What would I do with a pent-up horse with a beaver trap for a bridle who could beg like a toy poodle for a dog cookie? The saddle, on the other hand, was fairly nice for something commercially built in prison, as most of them are. It was worth at least five hundred dollars. Newly married with a baby, with the large reality of having to make ends meet, they were selling off those things that their former, single lives had consisted of, especially the horse whose feed was consuming money that could be better used to feed the family.

At least that's what it looked like from where I stood that day, for I knew that situation pretty well.

For us, though money was coming in better now, we certainly were not well off, but Indian rich as it were, which meant we could afford a little to help someone else who needed it. So I made them an offer. "The saddle looks pretty nice," I said. I could use a real saddle, for I was still busting my bottom on the chicken snare saddle I built for Juniper. "I tell you what, I'll buy the saddle for one hundred and fifty dollars and you keep your horse and sell him to somebody else, you'll make double that way."

But mysteriously they refused, "No, we can't do that. If you want the saddle, you have to take the horse. We'll throw in four bales of hay. You won't find a horse that can stand and dance in circles anywhere for this price."

For a couple of months now, people had been coming up into our place trying to buy Juniper after seeing how happy I was and how effortlessly and free we *coursed* alongside the asphalt on our way home from praying up at The Cross. Someone had astounded me by offering a thousand dollars, another fifteen hundred. One couple, a beautiful Black woman from Oklahoma and her Indian girlfriend, offered me eighteen hundred dollars if I'd sell Juniper to them along with all the "old time" tack! Including the three hundred dollars worth of hay I'd fed her since she'd come, that came to more than three times what I had spent "reanimating" the little mare. The wife was livid that I wouldn't even consider selling and making some good business out of that animal.

But Juniper had given all of us a lot of friendship and established some small degree of respect for us in the eyes of the locals. Though I knew she would soon be costing us a lot to keep, maybe even eat us into a debt, for she still colicked at least once every two months and probably always would, she was my sidekick, my friend, and so far my only handle on the goodness of the Wild-Flowering-Earth existence. I couldn't sell her.

But here, for one hundred fifty dollars, was a horse I could have, that danced like a small dog begging for a biscuit, a good saddle, and four bales of hay.

Though I could tell, unlike Juniper, I would probably never be a "friend" with Wiener, I was eager to own a paint and maybe I could work with him and get him going as a good, young, riding horse that someone might want to buy. He could even stand up and beg for a biscuit.

I had already begun to calculate how, if I could sell a cheaply purchased, non-fancy horse in four months or less for at least two and a half times what I'd paid for him, I would always make enough to cover the feed plus a large profit since the sweat was all mine and the joy of slowly welding our beings into a team made the money I'd bring in "tuning up" a rougher horse to pay Juniper's hay bill, a bill I could probably pass through the family review board.

So I bought the saddle. A saddle which came with four bales of orchard grass (good for horses) and a flashy, fiery parade paint horse on the side!

It was all a little suspicious. The two of them were happier that saddle and horse were leaving than they were about the one hundred and fifty dollars cash. They were in such a hurry to make it all happen that upon learning I'd have to arrange to borrow the use of a horse trailer and would return to pick up the horse in a couple of days, JoJo began raising a makeshift stock rack off my truck bed with spare lumber and sticks, wire, and bolts laying around their place, intending to load up and tie Wiener directly into my truck bed so I could haul him away right then and there.

In my early days none of us had ever seen a horse trailer and all horses had been trained to jump into pickup truck beds and then transported to far away ranch duties and so forth. It was now against the regulations, just as it had become for people riding in truck beds on the highway, which as a boy was the number-one, standard transportation of all New Mexicans.

Like a pro, Wiener jumped right in and let JoJo tie his head over the cab. I was amazed but terrified this crazy horse might decide to smash the boards and jump to his death on the highway somewhere as we moved the fifty miles or so to our camp.

To the contrary, his eyes squinted in the wind, ears forward, like a cattle dog riding in the bed, he seemed to immensely enjoy the ride, bugling importantly at the top of his lungs at every stop, as if to urge us back into motion, and wouldn't stop yelling until we did.

Every time some car with its windows down blasting music pulled alongside, my truck would commence to rock and jitter from left to right as Wiener, pumping his front legs, took up the rhythm, and together, truck and horse, rocked back and forth rolling down the road until the music was out of range. Truly he was a parade horse. Never in my life, with all the things I'd ever done, or thought, all the languages I'd ever spoken, and everywhere I'd been, did I ever expect to own a horse that danced to human music and could bounce around on his hind legs like a terrier begging for a bone. This little paint was starting to grow on me, though I only ended up with him to get the saddle.

Juniper wasn't crazy about the gelding when I let him into her corral, laying down the law with a barrage of nasty squeals and well aimed mule kicks to his chest until he retreated into the fence, which was all to be expected. But they eventually settled down into the horse ritual of delineating who was tall, who was short, who came first, who came second, who ate what, when, where, and how and life was as good as it could be. Juniper was even fiercer than the little paint! Horses always surprise.

The family on the other hand loved Wiener. To my great relief, unlike the first time when I went for eggs and came home with Juniper, they kept congratulating themselves on having such a pretty horse, admiring the good saddle, and the sweet smell of the pine stock racks on the truck made from recently milled mountain lumber.

Though I'd inherited that beaver-trap-looking, steel, snout-clamp of a bridle with Wiener, I was determined to accustom this little paint to a more pleasant type of head-rig.

I would "bring out" the obvious beauty and brilliance of this powerful little horse, letting all the trivial smell of his past drop away like a husk to reveal the grand being hidden inside him.

So, naïvely, saddling and bridling him with a light bridle and a mild snaffle bit, I mounted, intending to let him take us up and down the little piece of road that ran from our camp to the highway past the river.

Crossing the stream, he took the water like a tank, and once on the other side he starting marching and prancing, trying to break loose to run, which movement was only intensified as I tried to rein him in, hoping thereby to turn him back down the rise, back through the stream, intending to run the edge off of him, up the same abandoned logging road I'd "trained" Icicles on, albeit now in the dry summer.

But it was not to be. For the more pressure he felt on the bit, whether turning or stopping, the more adamantly he forged ahead, his velocity increasing until, getting his hinder parts beneath us, he finally leapt out straight onto the asphalt and bolted straight west, down the lone highway with no regard to any signal I attempted, moving at a phenomenal speed right down the middle line of the road that would only be matched years later by an even faster horse. Foolish people in cars tooted and screamed thinking I was intentionally riding on the highway or stupidly thinking the horse might obey their honking and mysteriously yield to what they felt was their car's superior right to "their" road, but this little paint was not running out of fear or because of anything I wanted.

Knowing well that if he slipped, jumped, or stumbled any small amount on the worn pavement we would washout and my survival would be unlikely in any configuration of his bone-sundering trajectory because we were moving out of control and into the wind, unarmored, at a minimum speed of forty-five miles per hour, which was increasing by the second. Even if I could have pulled his head by force to one side to slow him, we most likely would have tumbled to our deaths; so like life, I decided to learn to ride what he was handing me, instead of trying to gain control over that which my hand had no power. I decided to ride him, instead of trying to stop him.

But, my friends, let me tell you, we were really moving. Those who knew me, or knew what they were seeing, pulled over and watched from stopped trucks making room for our scary run. All these knew that this horse and I, who showed no signs of tiring, were headed down a hill on the asphalt straight toward a cattle guard, where we would no doubt crash for sure, shattering into bits.

But by instinct and with nothing to lose, I decided instead to put the peddle to the metal and began urging him with my heels and using the reins as a quirt to speed him up even more. Like a machine gun his poor hooves hammered the pavement, and like a bluebird flying over a dish drainer, that crazy fool dusted the cattle guard, flying clear over it at a full out run without even grazing it, losing not a single hair or hoof and without losing a beat continued his mad flight to who knew where at an unbelievable speed. Still on top and riding it out, I began breathing a little, and acting like we did this every day, and in that mode, at about three miles out, he slowed to a medium *coursing* roll, then to a gallop, then after another mile of that and two more cattle guards we entered the interstate, pulled onto the shoulder, where he dropped into an elegant canter at which point he finally started listening to his rider, as the semi's hurried past.

By now of course, it was obvious to me this horse's name was not Weiner but Winner! I'd misheard it. He was none other than a very highly practiced, very fast racing horse of the sandlot variety. At the speeds he was robotically achieving, he'd probably won somebody a good amount of cash on the private, underground, racing circuit so popular in the west and especially New Mexico, where it was illegal but carried out secretly. No doubt he had been targeted by some group of angry gamblers who, having lost so heavily, conspired either to steal him, report his owner to the authorities, or vindictively destroy him—as it had so often tragically played itself out in other cases of which we had all heard about.

This explained the urgency of his present owner to part with the horse and saddle, to avoid his discovery by either the authorities or their gambling enemies.

Though utterly sweat-soaked, head to tail, withers to toe, and totally *in hand* by now, I nonetheless didn't want him to slow too quickly or take too much pressure off his heaving sides and agile back, so I kept him moving at a light canter for a mile more moving onto the soft earth off the highway and through a fence-break rode him down a small track I knew to a gash toward the creek and following its bed made our way back toward our camp through the hills.

After five miles of all out pounding on hard pavement anyone would assume his feet were finished, wrecked, shredded, and concussed beyond imagining from all the hard hammering, so I sought a route of wet, creekside sand to slowly take the fire out of his feet for a mile, after which I set him at a walk the remaining five miles back to the camp.

Then I took a deep breath.

He really was a good horse, for he brought me home still alive on top, he never stumbled, he didn't founder or lame up in any way, and wisely didn't even try to drink for another three hours and was absolutely none the worse for it all when he did, ready again by morning for whatever we'd throw at him.

Most racing horses are made to run *on the bit*, in other words, instead of pulling up to a stop when you tug the bit with the reins, they just understand that as a signal to increase their speed forwards. I guessed that was the reason they had used such a severe contraption to stifle his run, for without it he would not have risen up to beg for the biscuit, but only run like hell for the money.

But the following morning I saddled him and rode him straight up a mountain for a couple miles, after which we glided nicely through the world just as calm and beautiful as I pleased.

One needed only to remember, if a snaffle mounted bridle was on his head he would read your signals to win a race. But if you had a bridle fitted with no bit at all but a simple braided rawhide pencil *bozal* noseband, you could ride him like a trained palfrey. And if a parade was what you wanted, riding with a headstall mounted with the same noseband and a bit as well would change all the signals and cause him to shoot up like a beagle begging for a bone, dancing around like a tame fool.

Two horses now I owned, a little red and a little paint, and each one of them I rode daily with my new saddle.

Because I hadn't liked the name Wiener, I never told anybody about it. Everybody in our camp called him Little Pinto, which almost stuck, but one day all the young neighboring mountain kids, returning from watching movies at a rich Native American neighbor's house, came running in yelling that I should name this able little pinto a Japanese name they'd picked up watching the *Karate Kid*.

They all loved this horse now, not only because he was a classic "Indian pony": all painted, with wild eyes, flowing mane, and sailed like a hero-bird over cattle guards, but because he was now locally famous for his five mile highway sprint. He needed a hero name, so they all started calling him Shindai, and it stuck.

And strangely Shindai immediately knew his name. If someone even whispered, "Shindai" fifty feet away, this little paint would spin around and stare expectantly at that person. So, Shindai he became.

When I asked what Shindai might mean translated into English, all the kids yelled that Pat Morita had told the Karate Kid it meant something like "legacy" or maybe "honor" in Japanese. Not speaking Japanese I took them at their word and because they loved the horse and Shindai liked his name and Shindai had a sound that matched his offbeat, wild-hearted willingness, Shindai became the name of a horse that could fly over cattle guards, could outrun the wind, and dance like a terrier begging for a biscuit to the music of a band.

Only two months had passed since he'd come to us and, with the right head gear, anyone could ride him. I was astounded; I'd bought him to fix up and sell and now he'd grown on me so much, I didn't want to let him go.

Chapter 10

Twin Beds

Overnight, Shindai had become something of mystical celebrity. The increasing knots of visitors that seemed to be all of a sudden frequenting our place identified our scene with Shindai's magical presence, as if he was somehow part of the medicine and ceremonies we made, on behalf of the people. Our cultural life and the beautiful land was all tied up in their minds somehow with the crazy-eyed, mythological, little "Indian Horse."

In my capacity as a Native doctor, clients came to see me, mostly in the early mornings. As our reputation grew, these clients also started bringing along family members or trusted friends who would wait patiently with our people in the camp or visit my horses while I worked with their friend or relative inside until we emerged from the "other world" around eleven in the morning.

For these people our camp was a bubble of other-world-ness, something from maybe two hundred years before their world, or a thousand after, and at least three thousand miles away from modernity's harsh spell of mediocrity. People began visiting us just to escape their own selves and the tiny, humdrum, choreographed existence they were stuck living in far away cities.

For some, just a courteous welcome and a drink of fire-cooked coffee, or a mug of home grown *atole*, seated in the smoke of our cooking fires, listening to our incessant jokes in a Native tongue, watching the antics of a famous, dirty-paint horse with crazy eyes beneath the sweet smelling firs and pines, above a gurgling *rito*, was in some ways a cure in and of itself.

Considered as a whole, most of these increasing numbers of visitors accompanying my clients were fairly respectful. After all, their presence in our camp came to them as a treat given by a sick friend or relative seeking life and alleviation for whose wellbeing I dedicated the other half of my own existence when I wasn't taking care of my family or suppling horses.

All these daily visitors were good for the family, for being tribal people and used to constant interpersonal village repartie, our life in the hills was a little isolated, but for me, because I was so integrally wound up with everyone's trouble, it was a little too crowded. But no matter, for when my work was done, by the afternoons, I could quietly move off and away from the crowds on the back of either Juniper or Shindai. Drinking in the motion, the weather, and the wind, the horses and the hills would re-flesh whatever part of me had been gnawed out of my being by the unconscious greed of these little bunches of city people.

The visitors we had to watch out for were a certain cadre of presumptuous waifs, who seemed to always attach themselves to Dolores on her return trips from the laundromat!

In her Native lakeside village of Atitlán the washing of the family clothing was not just about getting things clean, it was a personal event and more: a kind of communal institution. Anywhere from seventy-five to six hundred girls, young maidens, middle-aged women, and matrons lined up daily, shoulder to shoulder, in long lakeside chains, behind their family's traditionally owned *Chjembel* or basaltic clothes scrubbing stones. Dolores, like all the lakeside Mayan women had been used to doing all her socializing, rumor gathering and mongering, opinion crafting and unofficial ordinance forming, news-gathering and proliferation in this gigantic, long-established, Indigenous, multi-aged troop of women whose wild, constant, bubbly chatter was a sound not unlike the raucous calls of the lake's population of water birds. This phenomenon had given rise to the designation of the Tzutujil as The Bird People by all other Indigenous highland villages.

The intact boldness and unabashed decibel intensity of that massive, cacophonous chorus of simultaneous gossiping and joking was quite daunting and no male would dare venture there uninvited for fear of being heckled or so artfully and intelligently satirized until he was melted down to the size of a fish egg for his audacity.

Nonetheless, washing clothing was also a kind of aboriginal Mayan parliament where a lot of issues were seriously aired. All the village thought-trends were galvanized behind those washing rocks as the woman beat their family's clothing free of smoke, crud, and the husk of time past to reveal the renewed, hand-woven cloth beneath, which shined like the seed of the present in whose beauty all the village clothed themselves in their tribal identity as Tzutujils. But there were times when the women definitely beat the hell out of their clothes on the rocks, getting a lot of anger out of their system and making a lot of seriously binding decisions.

But in America, there were machines: machines for gossiping, machines for moving, machines for cooking, and machines for washing everything. What did *people* actually do, Dolores would ask, besides wait, depressed, for machines to finish *their* doing.

In a sad but concerted effort to continue as a real "non-machine person", Dolores still preferred to wash our clothing in a laundromat where machines did all the slapping and sloshing. As bleak and depressing as laundromats all seemed, Dolores could still keep up a steady and friendly banter with other customers, the bulk of which, at least in Santa Fe, were out of town travelers, tourists. Others, servants to the rich, were often actually Central American Indian women.

Visitors who found this Indian lady fascinating not infrequently followed her home and took their place at our cooking fires. A lot of interesting friendships came about in this way, people with whom we usually got on fairly well. But more often than not "kids on the road" would invite all their comrades and move in, availing themselves of our "cool scene" and devouring our free food and constant attention, eventually forcing one of us to break our own law and ask them to leave after a week or so.

Our pride and dignity depended on our unwavering willingness to welcome a guest, even if they were uninvited or turned out to be dishonorable and spoiled, oblivious to the burden their presence caused their benefactors. It would kill our identity and feeling of worth to ask anyone to leave or close our doors in anyone's face. We would become just as lost and vacuous as those who exploited us if we turned any of them away. Our capacity to royally bestow hospitality on any and all visitors was our only real wealth.

One evening Dolores returned from Santa Fe with a vivacious, young Japanese lady and her eighteen-year-old brother who had followed her home from the laundromat and basically moved right in. They made themselves peculiarly useful, the older sister Hizuru cured our problem with abusive visitors by chasing them off when they'd overstayed their welcome so we didn't have to! Very un-Japanese really, but since we weren't her relatives and she wasn't ours, it worked out perfectly. Of course she was only protecting their own interests: the "project" of learning from us Indigenous people in their year-long, family-funded, educational, hitchhiking adventure.

The family loved these two because they cooked some great meals for us, off and on, and the girls got very frequent Shiatsu treatments, foot rubs, and giggled all the way through being walked on up and down. We all sang at night, trading songs and instruments. They were a lot of fun in a way and tried at least to help us in the work of our daily lives.

But after two weeks, one day brother and sister had a running row in Japanese that ended with Hideo abandoned at our place, lost to the world, while his sister stomped off to parts unknown to broker some big business in the States, on behalf of their father in Japan.

We had no idea what they had argued about but, after a while, we put it together that little brother thought the spoiled life of eternal parties and carefree existence they enjoyed was a hypocrisy and they would never become real people by always wielding their family's vast money, instead of really laboring to deserve their lives. Big sister thought he was being stupid and naïve and left him to fend for himself to teach him a lesson, while she went off to manage a famous Japanese, new-age musician and buy up old restored Cadillacs for their father, who had buyers in Japan.

Hideo was a big, two hundred pound, unblemished, soft, very hip, courteous, handsome kid with a rather sad, hound-dog-like manner and a deep voice, whose large hands had never seen one minute of work, which he kept buried in the pockets of his big-city, high-fashion, hitchhiking trousers.

His name meant hero in Japanese, but the boy having never had to think for himself was lost without his sister who had called all the shots and had run their life like an aristocrat's working vacation as they went among the "common" people.

This young man, who we'd never seen get out of bed before one in the afternoon, was now up with the sun and had assigned himself the position of my personal assistant. Hideo began tagging along behind me like a big puppy, following me in my every task, coat collar up, hands in the pocket, looking very significant and forlorn, very hip and very Japanese, very poetic.

While I turned the crank of the mill to grind the grain for our geese and chickens, he was there watching. "How are you today, my friend?" I asked.

Enunciating very clearly and slowly "I find myself, profoundly depressed" was all he would say. When I offered to let him help me turn the grinding crank, he smiled a bit. He was very clumsy, but he figured it out.

After we finished and tripped down the embankment trail to feed the birds, when I asked him to help scatter the grain, he accidentally dumped most of the grain in a pile on his feet, but smiled when the birds pecked the cracked corn off his shoes.

"I find myself, profoundly depressed" was all he kept saying whenever asked what he wanted to help with.

But after a week of this, all the children within a couple miles would ride the school bus to our place after school to sit and stare at Hideo.

"Martín," Hideo hailed me, while together we carved some new prayer sticks for one of my ceremonies on the morrow.

"Why are all these children staring at me?"

"Somebody told them that you are a Japanese relative

of Bruce Lee, they think you're a Karate expert and a movie star!" I explained that this was New Mexico and of course it was inevitable that rumors would fly afar and mutate beyond all imagining.

Kung Fu and karate movies were all the rage then in the 1980's and Hideo and his sister certainly did look and act like movie celebrities. While Hideo might resemble a big, bulky Japanese style Kung Fu celebrity, his demure sister actually was versed in a lot of Japanese martial arts and meditations, whereas Hideo was mostly "profoundly depressed" and extremely uninterested in fighting, or success.

So, while Hideo continued to follow me around like a little kid everywhere and tried to be a help to me in my daily chores, he too was followed every afternoon by several little kids who wanted to do everything he did, while I was off riding until the evening.

He literally became "Hideo", their hero. When the chores were done, the healing sessions and ceremonies had come to a close and I'd ridden off on Shindai, like Ferdinand the Bull, Hideo always stayed behind and just played sad songs for the kids on the flute that he and his sister had made under my tutelage. The songs were beautiful in their own way and one day, unbeknownst to me, the "Karate Kids" convinced him to help them make their own flutes as well.

That day they didn't see us as we came down the last cliff, so I pulled up on Shindai to peep at them, unseen from afar, hidden behind a Ponderosa trunk. We stood as still as bedrock, watching, as Hideo, finally with a smile on his face and relatively animated, had every eight and ten-year-old with a flute, hollowed out and fitted with mouthpiece and fingerholes from some Elderberry stalks I had left to dry up in the fork of a tree.

We waited and secretly watched and within the hour he had them all tweeting away. And then, like Musashi in the cave, Hideo, on his own flute, played breathy *shakuhachi*-like riffs that no doubt only reinforced the children's conviction that he was indeed a Japanese, martial artist, monk, movie hero.

Sneaking out from behind our tree, Shindai and I approached very quietly, in an old warrior method I'd learned as a kid, and with no one noticing, for a joke, we spooked them all from behind, to their great screaming delight.

"Shindai, hey Shindai," all the little ones yelled, "it's Shindai."

"Look, Sensei." (They'd learned to call Hideo Sensei from the movies!)

"Shindai is here," totally elated by the fact that their flute playing, movie star, karate hero and their other hero Shindai, the horse whose name meant "Honor" in Karate-Kid-Japanese were all here together at the same time.

"Can you believe it Sensei Hideo, you and Shindai are here together?!"

"Oh, hello Martín," Hideo spoke low and a little contrite, "I hope I was not incorrect to use your tools and the stalks to make flutes with these guys. I hope you will forgive me."

"I will forgive all of you only if you play Shindai a song together." So they did. Hideo had them all play a single note in a marching rhythm while he played a riff over the top. It was actually rather stirring, and as I had hoped...

Shindai, of course, started rocking back and forth on his front legs, dancing to the song, which caused Hideo—for the first time ever that we'd seen or heard of—to burst out laughing, until he bent over trying to stifle his chuckling, still trying to play his flute.

When we all had a little less laugh bubbling up in us and Hideo could again speak, he spoke a little louder and for once not like a sad moose, "Okay, Martín, now please tell me why is this horse named Shindai?"

The little kids explained all at once about how they'd given Shindai his exalted name which in Japanese meant honor.

"I've been wondering why this beautiful horse had the name of Shindai. I thought maybe it was an Indian word."

"Well kids, the word for honor in Japanese comes out as *bushido*. Can you say *bushido*?" Hideo instructed.

All the kids yelled "Bushido, Bushido, Bushido."

"Sensei Hideo, then what does Shindai mean in Japanese?"

"Well I don't know where you found this word" Hideo apologetically related, "but in the Japanese language today, the word Shindai means a bed!"

The kids all yelled: "Bed, Bed, Bed!"

It was my turn to howl and laugh till I cried. All this time I'd been riding a horse named Bed?!

There were horses named Domino, Ace, Pistol, Periscope, Dynamite, Thimble, Bullet, Dream Catcher, Swizzle, Rooster, Hatchet, Chico, Rascal, Reamer, Axle, Dodge, Anvil, Eightball,

Dreamer, Dolly, Link, Ramrod, Cannonball, Paul, Ruby, Bugle, Pie Plate, Dingus, Singer and Sack. But I'd never heard of a horse named Bed! And here I was riding around on a horse named bed in Japanese. But then again Bed was better than Wiener!

Hideo, on the other hand, discovered he was born to become a teacher of little kids. They loved him and his noble, hound dog demeanor. Every day, if they could escape their homework and homes, increasing numbers of little kids poured into our place after school searching for Hideo to teach them what the day before Hideo had learned from me or the family in our camp, always ending his "lessons" with a meditation and an orchestrated flute ensemble, which they took as the beginning of their "martial arts" instruction.

Hideo, of course, knew not one move of Aikido or Karate, but unexpectedly discovered he loved teaching little ones how to do what he was now immensely happy learning himself.

A week or so before his sister would mysteriously reappear—when he would inform her he was returning to Japan to become a grade school teacher and a *shakuhachi* student and forcing her to buy his ticket home—I finally got Hideo on Juniper while I rode Shindai, the Bed. He only fell off twice and bumped his head on a tree branch once, but after a couple of afternoons, like the rest of us, he fell in love with riding out in the bush and got fairly good at it.

I'd rationalized the expense of our feeding Shindai by telling myself I'd bought him to train and sell for a profit, to purchase feed for Juniper, but had conveniently forgotten all that when he turned out to be so grand and interesting.

But, one evening as I came riding little, crazy-eyed "Bed" in from the old Pueblo ruins to our south, while crossing the little bend of asphalt road back into our place, a small, white, Blazer-type car was stationed at the entrance.

The occupants were a local-looking Spanish lady and her friendly, heavy-set husband who followed me home and watched while I put Shindai away and fed him.

Hideo was playing flute on our cabin steps, while our resident mocking bird traded riffs with him from up on the cliff behind.

This couple in the car got out, introduced themselves, and hung on the fence admiring Shindai. They wanted to show me an enlarged snapshot they had brought along.

"You'll probably be interested in seeing this."

And there he was, a picture of Shindai all togged out in a harness, combed out, spiffed up, hitched to a miniature covered wagon. A million thoughts raced through my head, the most salient of them, that Shindai had indeed been a stolen, unbranded horse and these people had come to claim him.

"Well what do you think about that?" they cheerfully asked. "How long ago was this picture taken?" I said, figuring they would say a couple of years back.

"When did we take this, Ed?" Minerva asked.

"At that parade in Albuquerque."

There it was, Shindai actually had belonged to these nice people and was a parade trained horse, obviously stolen and then sold off quick to a fool like me. I was going to lose Shindai back to his rightful owners. My heart sank.

At this point Hideo had walked quietly to where we stood and peered over my shoulder to see the picture.

"Whose horse is that?" Hideo said in his shy tone.

"Ours," the two blurted.

"Wow, he looks just like Martín's horse here."

"Yeah, exactly. That's why we've come to talk, because we have a cabin down in Pecos and every weekend for the last four months we've been noticing this little paint from the road and seen you folks riding him and just thought we'd try to talk you into selling him to us."

"He's the identical twin of our little wagon pony and we want to put together a matching team to ride in rodeo half-times and parades!"

The horse in their photograph had to be Shindai because in every respect he looked exactly the same. He had the same dirty paint markings, same long mane parted and hanging in the same places, same color of the same long tail, same color hooves, same height, the same crazy eyes.

Then Hideo spoke again:

"Except for the fact that Shindai is a man and your horse is a girl, you can't tell them apart."

And he was right. I hadn't even noticed; Shindai was a gelding and the horse in the photo was a mare!

They were otherwise identical.

Their horse had come from northern Mexico and Shindai probably *had* been stolen from where, from who, and when, who knew?

Ed and Minerva worked on me for a month to sell them Shindai. They didn't care that he didn't know yet how to be harnessed or how to pull, they would teach him, and of course I knew they could do it.

Like Hideo, the little lost brother who became a hero teacher for the local kids, the little pent-up paint Wiener had become Shindai, the hero and mascot of our way of life. Remembering how I'd promised myself to never sell an unwanted horse, but to always sell only the best and most special and how I'd also promised the family Shindai was come to us specifically so I could knock off his rough edges and sell him for a profit in order to feed Juniper through the winter and maybe be able to purchase another horse to do the same, without having to dip into any money needed to support the family, I, in a rare instance of bitter-sweet, rational thinking capitulated to Ed and Minerva when they upped the ante to three thousand dollars they were willing to give us for this funny, little horse that I'd paid nothing for, who could dance to music, and beg for a biscuit, outrun the wind, fly over cattle guards, and whose name actually meant bed. A week after Shindai left us for his new home seventy miles south in Corrales, Hizuru had reappeared driving one of her Father's nineteen, newly purchased, 1950's and 60's, restored Cadillacs and was come to give Hideo a ride to the airport.

The final day when Hideo was to leave, the whole world of loud, little, mountain kids and their families came to sing and play their flutes for him. It was a beautiful, simple feast but a little sad. All their heroes were leaving. The kids hated to see Shindai gone, though everyone knew he'd gone to a very good home and now Hideo would be gone that evening too, who they would miss even more. We loaded him up with gifts and sang and ate, then wept. Hideo got into the fancy old Coupe de Ville with his fancy, rich sister at the wheel. As a final parting memento, through the window, I handed Hideo a photo that Ed had taken of Shindai and his twin cousin both harnessed up in front of their little parade wagon with Minerva in the driver's seat holding the reins, with *both* horses standing up on their rears, both of them looking all the world like two big dogs begging for biscuits! Who had trained who?!

Grinning like a sloth, Hideo got back out of the car and hugging me and the family again with teary eyes held up the photo to show the crowd and then with a choked up voice yelled, "Look, everybody! Twin Beds," and in a cloud of dust, laughter, and tears they drove off into their new lives and out of ours.

Chapter 11

Ta Shunk

Heartened by the economic good fortune enjoyed from the reluctant and saddening sale of Shindai and to help dissolve a little of the grief his absence caused in our camp, some of the "Shindai money" went to the purchase of more horses who I also intended to work up and sell for some small profit, as I had the "Bed".

I was in no way what could be termed a horse trainer. I just couldn't get enough of moving over the natural earth on horseback, so I took any pretense that made that kind of riding a reality, especially if it helped feed the family, so they didn't think I was just having a good time, which of course, I was.

After Shindai, six other horses had come and five had already been worked and sold in less than five months.

My proclivity for discovering solid but under-appreciated grade horses cheap seemed to be holding up. In almost every instance, I bought from individuals or regular family people who mostly had one tame horse who they could no longer rationalize feeding, or whose college bound daughter had lost interest, or who were over their heads trying to ride too much of a horse.

I only bargained for horses where, with a little vision, one could discern in each one some unique quality, or some sense of humor, or a willing demeanor about which their previous owners had no time or maybe didn't really care.

To be sure, all these backyard horses had their human-enforced weirdnesses and habits, but ignoring all their acquired dodges and avoidance schemes, mostly I'd just saddle and ride each one, hard and honestly, as much as they could handle, increasing the distance and effort by the day, until their rough edges shed away over the weeks. This was heaven for me, as all I did was ride through the mountain cliffs, around pillars of stone, around bears, through creeks, and hard up steep log skids and watch each horse for their unique talent to start pushing through to the surface. You couldn't force their singular talents to emerge, you just kept them working and waited for it to happen, each in their own way. When it happened though, it was best to continue in a matter-of-fact way, slowly encouraging that singular thing each of them had, coaxing it out of its hidden seed husk, without rushing, until it came to the surface, sprouting into tangible reality in a way where the horse couldn't wait to try it again, day by day, transforming into themselves all on their own, I just provided the place and a little push.

My experience with a lot of trainers and official horse sellers was that they generally tended to be as squirrelly as the horses they peddled. Like used car salesmen, they would say anything for a sale, so I never bought any horses from "experts" but only from regular, struggling people who loved their horses but couldn't keep them.

It stood to reason, given the duplicitous nature of trade in civilization, most people who did what I was trying to do never actually sold a good horse, because if a horse was really good, ninety percent of the time, dealers either kept them out of the market or had a list of elite buyers for a given type of horse, with no need to advertise.

A truly great horse is like a good frying pan, you can't actually buy one. You have to find one that might eventually become one, then slowly cook and cure them into shape.

Horses can be mechanically trained to carry out a surprising array of maneuvers, but great horses are not those mechanically produced. Like cast iron frying pans they have to be slowly heated, cooled, cured, heated, and cooled together with their riders such that over time and use, they both become indispensably useful to each other.

Cooks don't usually sell a well cured, ready to use, frying pan any more than a dedicated horse owner sells a horse that's actually all fixed up and working really well.

The animals that people who know horses generally sell are either those nobody can handle or those who don't live up to their owner's preconceived desires. Although my definition of a good horse had nothing to do with horse shows or spectator performance rides, eventing, racing, or rodeos, I still wanted to sell only vital and good horses. As naïve as I've always been, I didn't think a world made of economically-successful liars and rip-off artists was going to help the Earth want to keep us humans on as tenants or did anything to keep alive the reality of the true goodness of horses beyond modern civilization's limiting definition of what was meant to be a horse by promoting over-specialized, neurotic performers with crumbling physiques.

The last five horses had sold rather easily, one person even buying two. This brought in a welcome addition to the hard-earned income I gleaned from my morning clients and the occasional sales of my art, but it also tremendously bolstered the legitimacy of the time and energy I expended working horses in the eyes of a wife who saw the financial risk of feeding a half-dozen horses as a potential disaster, not to mention the ever present physical risk.

Most likely the ease with which these horses sold had more to do with the romance of our old-style, out-of-time, smoky camp and the open-faced aura of vagabond joy and spiritual liberty each horse emanated as we slalomed through the heart of the Holy Earth, Her land, through Her rivers, around Her trees, than it did with how well the horses were trained or how good their "manners" actually were.

I often wondered if those people who purchased my horses were not half way hoping that the freedom of a horseback life and our seemingly unfettered, self-determined existence, away from bosses and stop lights, would not somehow be magically included with the horses they got from me! I would have wished it so, if I'd had the power to bestow it.

On the other hand, the sixth horse in the group was a totally different creature and not the kind of animal I'd ever purposely sought out and as it panned-out, almost impossible to sell. None other than a registered Paint Horse, he was the product of commercial manipulation of horse genes to obtain a fancy coat color pattern, who'd been rather slyly maneuvered into my life by an impostor: a professional horse broker skilfully camouflaged as a bona fide human being.

Posing as a landlord, who'd been given the horse in lieu of past due rent by a fictitious family destroyed in a terrible divorce before they'd all broken up and disappeared, he pretended the sale of horse was his only recourse to recoup the lost rent.

Though suspiciously cheap for what he was I bought him anyway 'cause the horse was smiling at me and charmingly pretty. I knew in my blood the whole thing was strange and something was wrong.

Later on, it would become obvious that this handsome, square standing, photogenic, overo gelding had been sold and repossessed over and over again in a barely legal, but unethical, ruse developed by some horse dealers, the same commonly practiced by used car dealers, where in order to get the most money out of a good-looking, but otherwise unsellable, not so rideable, but "fancy" brand of horse, they preyed on the fears of inferiority of ladder climbing people trying to appear well-off, who were living beyond their means, falsely leading them to believe they could really upgrade their appearance and acceptance into a higher social standing by owning and boarding a blooded horse in a fancy stable.

Once the horse was found to be too difficult and the buyer couldn't sell him, the original seller, not willing to take the horse back, once the client defaulted on the payments, actually repossessed this poor animal, kept the down payment and sold him over again. This was repeated again and again with each new gullible buyer until the horse had made as much money as another of his type that really functioned. Then, at the end of the trail, the horse was finally sold off cheaply to anyone who'd buy him or, if not, auctioned for slaughter. That's what I had bought.

For a heartbroken, multi-blooded, fish-out-of-water, type man who had a different vision of what living meant, I thought our family was doing pretty well, considering. But I was often a sucker for a beautiful horse, especially a Paint. Every once in a while you catch a funny fish, no matter what they look like, and there was no throwing this one back once we realized what he was. My own big head got me hooked by this fish and I got pulled into a swamp of business hypocrisy of the type I swore I'd never go near and I came out thoroughly soaked.

It didn't take long to realize I'd finally met and had been expertly swindled by exactly what I didn't want to become. But then again Ta Shunk, as we called him, was still a live being and it wasn't really his fault. There he was staring back at me expectantly, out of the shadow of a Douglas Fir, all covered in dust, a cowbird on his back, in his new, very unmodern corral. Being a city boy and unused to mountainsides, Ta Shunk had already successfully tripped himself and tossed his spiffy, inept self to the ground twice, cross-locking his legs in the rails in a rather ingenious fashion so that he was ridiculously immobilized until I maneuvered him loose.

Juniper didn't know what to do with him any more than I did. He didn't smell exactly right: a little sharp and not entirely horse like. His mane had been trimmed and his long forelock never got tangled and looked like it had been combed by a Christian mom on Sunday. He always stood squared up like he was getting his picture took for a catalog. His veins stood out like an Arabian horse's and his fur was sleek, but had not been renewed by growing long in a hard winter, shed, and regrown.

Like the people that must've engineered his parentage, he was obviously raised in cubicles and run around in covered arenas, for Shunk didn't have a single scar on him, had no herd instinct, and was horrified at Juniper's normal horse etiquette of sorting out pecking order by kicks and squeals.

As a matter of fact, after three months, I'd never even heard him whinny, which seemed strange. When he finally gave it a try, he was so unpracticed at that beautiful horse singing all real horses have, that he scared himself when he did let his whinny out sounding pretty much like a raw-voiced, cigarette-smoking, diner cook crossed on a donkey!

Of all the things that made him different from any other horse, or even any quadruped I'd ever come across, was the fact that when he moved he went more up than forward. Ladies and gentlemen, this crazy painted Shunk was a vertical horse.

Though catching him and saddling him was not too bad, he was so tense about it all that you could have bounced a hammer off his neck. When I finally climbed up on him, he stood as stiff and square as a dining room table.

When it came time for us to get going up into the forest trails he didn't really want to move and when he finally did it wasn't forward, or backwards, it was just up.

I don't mean to imply that he went into a frenzy of bucking, because he hadn't shown any fondness for biting, kicking, bucking, or rearing up, at least not while you were on him, but it was as if his feet had coil springs nailed onto all fours, for all he did was bounce up and down. As hard as he tried to go forward, and he really did try hard, his head would bob frantically up and down, his legs would pump away like pistons, his whole body bouncing with such effort that he dripped in sweat, but all just to travel almost six inches! He wouldn't walk, he didn't trot, and I couldn't get him to canter, he just kind of bounced along like a life-loving, moon-walking nerd with new tennis shoes jittering his way up the trail in a strenuous, teeth-jarring strut. But for all his incredible motion, noise, and effort he hardly made any progress forward.

I could've laid down on the ground and rolled up a hill sideways faster than this horse could move on the flat.

It wasn't that he wasn't rideable, 'cause you could easily get on him. He just wasn't "go-able".

The horse and myself were both covered in sweat, for it took as much effort to ride and coax this bobbing, wobbling, bouncing, jolting wonder as it took the horse to do it. Horses walk, trot, run, and canter along by nature from six hours after being born. I couldn't imagine what had happened that would have made this horse unable to freely move across the open land. It was unnatural and unhorse-like. It was as if his gears were stuck.

But not to be deterred, I saddled him and took him out each day and tried to find the secret that would get him to shift gears out of a bounce into walk or run. But both of us were exhausted after just a few days of this decidedly weird situation. I even tried dragging him behind Juniper on a long lead. He came along a little better, but still it was at the same idiotic, bouncing strut. And the worst part was that he smiled all the time and his hairdo never came uncombed!

After a month he was moving faster, but still continued with a practically unrideable jolt. I named his gait "The Jolt". So I rode him at a jolt, practically standing in the saddle. He turned and stopped wonderfully. But it seemed he just wanted to go up and up and up to the sky instead of forward.

I felt all my horses should be able to cross streams and puddles, learn to stand so you could open or close a gate, drag a rope, pack any kind of object, animal or tool, and, of course, ride up and let their rider open the rural route mailbox to check their post or to mail a letter.

The first time I bounced big, fancy Ta Shunk down to the little creek, he, like a lot of young horses, didn't want to get his feet wet. Some horses absolutely love water and these you have to watch a little bit as you enter a stream or a pond to cross because about midstream they will always try to sink down into the water and roll with you on. Others want nothing to do with standing water, going to great lengths to avoid even a tiny puddle. Most people think that is because horses see all the clouds and flying birds from the sky reflected in the puddle on the ground, where they shouldn't be. That might be so in some cases, but most horses who dislike ground puddles will generally even sneak up on their water tank to drink, because its written in their horse minds that for millions of years their ancestors have become welcome meals for all types of steppe lions, wolves, leopards, even crocodiles while a herd slakes their thirst at the water's edge. That part of a horse's neck behind their ears, is made vulnerable by their bending down to drink and a pack of predators could easily pounce and snap the spinal chord. Horses love drinking water so much that it's a trance-like event and they lose some of their wariness when drinking. Knowing this they wait and check around the water for a while before bending down to imbibe the euphoria of drinking water.

A potential enemy above them reflected in the water, or any sign of an actual enemy *in* the water, like a river croc, makes horses instinctually watchful when crossing water, but ironically this also slows them down enough to be easily pulled down by a meat eater hiding nearby.

When Shunk and I bumped up to the stream, he stopped stiff. When urged to enter, like a lot of horses, he thought it might be better to try and jump over the whole creek, which, with a running start, he could've mostly achieved, for the creek was a bare six or seven feet in width.

That was just fine with me, for I'd jumped lots of smaller streams on horses.

So I urged him on. He kind of crouched down, a bit like a stalking cat, trembling from side to side in excitement, then like releasing the trigger on a powerful spring, *bango,* up he sprang with a lurch so tremendous that for a moment it had me hoping he would finally make a measurable, forward motion. And up into the air we went with an impressive leap in hopes of crossing the stream, but when we landed with a thunk we were at least six inches behind where we had started from!

Shunk had jumped in reverse!!

I couldn't believe it. I'd never known a horse that could jump backwards on purpose. We tried over and over with me laughing all the way and each time getting farther and farther away from the stream. It was so funny I could hardly stay in the saddle for laughing so hard. The crazy horse couldn't jump forward like every other horse on earth, but he could actually jump backwards, covering more distance in less time than he could bounce and jitter forward. It was so nutty and unbelievable, and there he was, not the least bit disgusted with himself, but smiling proudly like a little kid having written his first sentence in reverse.

But, of course, rivers go with their own flow so why should I fight him? "This might be," I thought to myself, "where his secret opening might be hiding."

Still tickled and chuckling, I turned him backwards and got his butt lined right up to the very edge of the little creek, his tail hanging over the water. Then I urged him forward away from the creek and *kerplosh*, he leaped backwards, his hind feet landing square into the water, about a foot from the creek's edge.

From where we stood I once again caused him to leap forward and again he leapt backwards and landed right in the middle of the creek! We were in the water! He started to shake but didn't make any effort to leave the shallow creek, which was only two feet deep.

Slowly I got him to turn around and face the opposite bank, but he refused to strut forward to exit the water. So I turned him, facing upstream, and we marched gaily up the middle of the little *rito*, bouncing, and splashing water madly everywhere to our great delight.

After about one hundred feet of this, again I tried to talk him into exiting the water by moving forward to the opposing bank, but again he froze, so, I turned him and tried to exit the creek on the side we'd entered and he froze even worse.

Still laughing, both of us dripping like otters, I turned his butt to the stream side opposite and gave him the signal to jump and by God he jumped backwards, over and over until, backing by leaps, we exited the stream. I'd never met a horse so strange in my entire life. It took us a full half an hour to cross a six foot stream, jumping backwards.

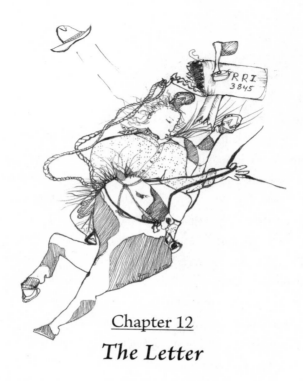

Chapter 12
The Letter

The winter following, no real mountain snow blessed us till March. But the wind was always on us, day and night, bitterly cold and constant. Though daily living and riding was a blustery and colder than usual affair, one afternoon in March, the wind driven out of the south-east came rushing up the Pecos escarpment and bottle-necked into Glorieta Pass roaring through the tall pines and firs, loud like an ocean surf, carrying the first real scent of snow that soon followed.

I was busy cleaning Ta Shunk's hooves, who was tied to the central barn post, preparing for a canyon ride in the first flurry of flakes, when a little flock of goldfinches, pine siskins, and juncos blown off target by a surprise gust grazed both Shunk's belly and back, helter skelter. Like any horse would, already crazed from the wind and the prospect of snow, he allowed the birds to spook him, which caused him to instantly rear up in fright, leaping so very high that he caught the side of his sleek painted head on the razor-edged, roof tin as he came down. His face was sliced cleanly from below his ear, all the way to the end of his back teeth, you could see his molars through the cut that ran eight inches down his face.

The snow turned to a windy blizzard as Shunk started to bleed into the white of the quickly drifting snow. Luckily, the cut had missed any big arteries. I ran to one of our tipis and like a mad man dug in my bags and found a pack of brand new number eight, Osborne glover's needles. I pushed back into the snowy wind up the hill to the pony, pulled out a couple long tail hairs from his tail and holding one in my teeth to keep the wind from hauling it off, I threaded the needle with the horse tail hair, which was made difficult because the temperature had dropped at least forty degrees and my hands were numbing up. Then snubbing poor Shunk's beautiful, hysterical head very tight to that rough timber to keep him from moving too much, but still dodging his striking front hooves, and with the cold as the only anesthetic, I sewed up that gash as fast as I could, considering all the movement, bad visibility, and wind. The whole slice closed up perfect and even, forming a neat, little, eight-inch, pucker seam just like a moccasin sewn using a pretty back stitch. The blood had pretty much coagulated, but I never thought my stitching would hold nor be clean enough to avoid a seriously ugly infection later on. Plus, how would he eat with that horrible wound inside his cheek?

By the time I untied his head it was dark and the snow was already eight inches deep with two foot drifts and piling higher by the minute. The blizzard was howling so fast and horizontal you could barely see your own hand, but by instinct I led the willing, wounded horse back to his corral, turned him loose and staggered down to our camp praying that I'd done the right thing considering no vet would be available for at least a couple days in this storm.

Some more down-to-earth horseiness had developed in Shunk and with that new vitality he learned to turn his butt to the wind and seek the shelter on the downwind side of the trees. When I fed him, he miraculously managed to negotiate the food I soaked for him on one side only, without compromising my sewing job, and never colicked for roughly chewed grass. He drank water fine and somehow swallowed. After three days, when his face swelled up, I washed and soaked it three times a day with hot plant medicine infusions of my own design. He learned to love the treatments, and day by day the swelling subsided, until the wound leaked only minimal proud flesh with no infection!

After six weeks when the crocuses of spring were back up out of winter's hard mind, Shunk's face just had a little line of white hair over the scar to show for the whole affair. He had healed very fast and well, as vital horses can, and was back eating better than normal. Taking out the stitches turned out to be more of a bullfight than putting them in, but in the end we both survived it all, neither one of us any the worse for the experience and life went on.

Though still hard on *my* teeth, Shunk's bouncy strut seemed to have mellowed a bit, either that, or I was just getting used to it. He still had only one gear, with three speeds: fast strut, slow strut, medium strut; no walk, no trot, no canter.

With the appearance of the solid ground of summer, I began taking him up to the asphalt to learn how to ride alongside traffic, where we also had our rural route mailbox planted on the north side of the road. To get there we still had to jump backwards through the stream, straighten up after we exited, and march on up to the road.

It was one thing for the horses I suppled to ride through the wild land and around bears, boulder fields, and over dangerous defiles, but totally more precarious to ride along the shoulders of highways with traffic where both of us had to contend with the unpredictable actions and moods of humans in charge of three-ton hunks of speeding metal and glass rushing by in two directions on one side and rows of signs and mailbox demons on the other. For a horse used to the normal hazards of nature, highway riding was an insane gauntlet of life-threatening monsters.

In my home-grown methods, I figured if together, a new horse and I the rider, could eventually ride alongside a frequented asphalt road for a couple of miles, past sinister mailboxes and signs in a relaxed but alert way, ready to dodge any drunken drivers who honked and yelled or threw beer cans at us, or any of those mean persons who swerved to scare a horse, or scared people who stupidly sat on their car horns to warn us away, then about one hundred important things been learned, confronted, and tolerated. But the greatest accomplishment was the horse's experience of the judgment of his rider to direct him through this unpredictable, nerve-wracking hell and safely back home again, which tended to inspire in the horse the hope that there were at least some humans in this world who could be trusted.

This riding between the demonic mailboxes and demonic automobiles was bad enough for most horses. But then came the unimaginable worst: the act of actually riding, point blank, up to one of the horrifying rural route mailbox demons on purpose, then opening his dangerous mouth, sticking "our" hand inside, retrieving crinkly, noisy, scary things (some scared me too), putting them in "our" shirt (a good horse thinks his rider is part of him or her, you should do the same), closing the mailbox's mouth with a suspicious plop, and then thankfully riding off *slowly* and *casually*, pretending we didn't want to get the Holy Hell out of there!

Though this may sound like no great achievement and a fairly simple maneuver, for a new horse there were at least nine seriously unsavory places in that simple event, each of which, on their own, was enough to unnerve any green horse. A green horse very intelligently perceived it all for what it was: a dangerous trap! Never mind that all these traps were strung together in some diabolical scheme causing an adrenal warning of sufficient urgency as to override any confidence a horse might have in a positive outcome and certainly "dangerous" enough to cause an otherwise sensible animal to tear off in uncontrollable flight to get as far away from that danger as possible, which in itself was rather dangerous on a paved highway.

While our family had only one, fairly large, unimposing, corrugated steel mailbox mounted on a square, rough-sawn, four foot post painted blue and buried well off the little asphalted road's gravel shoulder, there were places on that same road where as many as fifteen mailboxes of all different colors and dimensions stood, jammed together in a row, their strange varied necks craning out of the ground, their different sized heads in every color, all staring menacingly, like the misfit children of demons, ready to attack any horse riding along the road foolish enough to come within their range. Most horses are initially terrified of these rural route mailboxes.

I had found that once a horse actually became courageous enough to allow his rider to fetch his or her mail regularly, so many other things became easy to do, like opening and closing swinging gates while mounted, dragging logs behind on a rope, etc. For this reason I kept up at it until this friendly motion became routine.

But it was easy to understand a horse's misgivings about the mail, for I could still recollect as a tiny child having pretty much the same opinion of roadside mailboxes. For right at eye level, all three foot of me, the opening and closing of mailboxes had a bad sound, an ominous hollow grind, grate, creak, thud, and clunk. And just like flounder fish, they seemed unnatural, with both their eyes weirdly on one side of their head, eyes that stared back at me, never blinking, in the form of their owner's name and number stenciled on the upper left side.

That stiff, little, curly, finger-hold, clamp-thing on top of the front-facing door when it was closed looked all the world like a grumpy, old tongue hanging out of the vertical, doggy-froggy mouth of some scheming, predatorial beast who might snap at me at any second. Forget the red flag that could swing up to preside over the top on the right, angry and bristling, waving in the air like the fierce topknot of some monster ready to strike. Like a little horse, if my mother hadn't a firm hold on my little hand, I would have lost my nerve and bolted away as fast as my chubby little legs would've taken me.

Together, Shunk and I had gone to get the mail three times that week, for the family was waiting for a letter from an art gallery in Denver containing what we hoped would be a check for what they owed me in sales for a few of my paintings, which came to about six thousand dollars. Recently, a lot of the families who lived farther up in the hills had their mailboxes pilfered by some group of *rateros* who counted on nobody being near to see them at it.

Shunk and I had not yet dared to try and fetch out the mail from the box while mounted, it being all he could do to even ride within six feet of the box without trembling like a berry bush in the wind, so up till now I'd always dismounted, checked the box, remounted, and rode off on down the highway, to his great relief.

Then the day came when I thought he might be just about ready to ride close enough to let me try it from the saddle.

To accustom Shunk to the sound of the lariat slapping on the saddle, I usually had a calf rope tied up somewhere on the saddle, and today, instead using the normal rope strap off the horn, I just carelessly tied up the coil on the front latigos in front of my right thigh, and away we went.

After cheerfully "backing" through the creek, straightening out, and bouncing up the rise to the asphalt, we took a sharp left, bounced past the mailbox, turned around and then approached our big, old mailbox so it presented itself off our right, so, with the reins in my left hand, I could grab the mail with my right hand.

Shunk was wide-eyed and real tense about getting that close to that mailbox, his whole body turning hard as a stone when he heard those stiff rope coils slap against the hollow sound of the box. He almost jumped, but I talked to him and coaxed him into staying, then leaning over, I very slowly opened the box, and there, to my delight, laying like an oyster in the shell was the promised letter with my check!

The mailbox door was straight out, from which position the curly finger-pull fell right over the rope coils attached to the saddle.

Trying hard not to be overly excited, I reached into the box, intending to retrieve that much awaited letter and a bill with a clear cellophane window which crinkled when I touched it, causing Shunk to stiffen and pull away in fear from the box, for which movement I needed both hands to curb. So I left the letter and the bill in the box and half way closed the lid while I grabbed the reins with both hands and rode him back down the road a bit to calm him.

I deliberated whether or not I should just dismount, fetch the check and remount and call it all a pretty good day, but I knew if I let his lesson go at that he would always know we could always just let it go at that and so I decided to ride back up to the half opened box and try again.

But Shunk had been tipped off by that the crinkling inside the mail box, which meant that mailbox demon was alive and gurgling and no doubt cooking up something bad. It took all my patience, my rap, my heels, and not a little strength to cause this powerfully built, nervous, high strung horse to sidle back up to that box that had my six thousand dollar check just waiting there for me to retrieve it.

The halfway open door of the mailbox made it even more suspicious than ever, like a half open mouth getting ready to snap and as we tensely pulled alongside; Ta Shunk stared at it bug eyed with his beautiful, seal-colored and white painted head cocked sideways, ready to jump if that evil box should make any false move!

And damned if it didn't. For just as we got within inches, the mailbox, acting every bit like the malicious monster he was, dropped his half open mouth as if to bite, the half cocked door plopping down right over the bottom of the loose coils of that blasted lariat I had stupidly tied to the front of the saddle, and Shunk, no doubt to save us both, leapt straight up in the air, like he was so good at, and the little tongue-like, finger pull on the top of the lid hooked onto the rope as he leapt, pulling the slack out of the coiled rope, which slid across Shunk's skin hissing like a great snake, raising a little smell of burnt hair, which was not the least bit reassuring to him and only confirmed the obvious: that this evil mailbox was attacking!

So, as Shunk was coming down from the sky with me still on him, and before he even landed, with a tremendous loud crack, he gave that malicious mailbox what he had coming by laying a hind leg kick of such power and aim that he successfully bent that mailbox's mouth, causing the little finger-pull on the lid that had rudely grabbed our rope to be hammered completely onto the rope, bent around it in such a firm, perfectly riveted kink that we were now permanently attached to the mailbox.

I know he was just trying to save us when he decided not to listen to me and once again leapt into the air even higher, but this time even though the rope had spun out a few feet to the rear, it was still firmly tied to the front of the saddle, and with the mailbox attached to it, whenever we moved the mailbox's mouth moved. Because the rope was riveted to the mailbox door, when we jumped, the mailbox door jerked open then slammed shut with a *bam* and then opened up again, just like a monster snapping at us!

This was too much for the horse who was now utterly convinced of the evil intent of this mailbox who was snapping his jaws at him, while I, hoping the mailbox would continue to protect my check, kept trying to unsheath my knife to slice the leather ties that kept us fastened to this diabolic mailbox and maybe free us of its horrible snapping threat, calm down the horse, dismount and go get my damned check! (We really needed the money.)

But this was made impossible.

Because Shunk was now leaping and kicking, pitching and twisting so violently that it was all I could do to ride him out, much less grab my knife. With Shunk's every jump, that mailbox continued to loudly open, then shut and snap at us over and over until Shunk, in a moment of hysterical desperation, finally let loose a mule kick that landed square on the monster's neck, shearing the post upon which the mailbox was mounted, unwittingly liberating that mailbox monster and its post from the earth and freeing it to leap up wildly in the air, where still snapping, it then had the audacity to chase us down the road! With the mailbox raising a tremendous racket attached to our rope, dragging behind us right at our heels, between kicks and bucks, Shunk actually started moving down the road.

A lot of bystanders in trucks and cars had courteously pulled to the side of the road to give wide berth to Shunk's mythological battle with the mailbox dragon. We were in the middle of the asphalt now and heading west, Shunk frantically taking gigantic leaps forward, making legitimate progress for the first time in his life, but every time he did so the mailbox bumbled right along on that damned rope, causing Shunk to jump into the air higher, which caused the mailbox, still snapping, to jump higher still, straight up with us, flying right by my head, then when the rope jerked smashing loudly back to the ground, still right with us when we came down. Every time that monster got into range Shunk would flash out a limb and whomp that mailbox dragon good, each time radically changing its shape, but never succeeding in stopping him from pursuing us. The harder he ran the faster the mailbox pursued us.

Jump, clang, kick, bam, boom, clunk, rattle down, clang bam, down, bam all the way down the road. Shunk, who was fighting hard and wild, in the fury and confusion, mistook cars slowing down and going past as part of the same monster and succeeded in kicking out at least three headlights, not a few tail lights, and dented a couple of doors. While the cars in that onslaught sensibly retreated and pulled over, that evil mail box was relentless, he never gave up but just kept coming. The ties on the saddle just wouldn't snap, the rope wouldn't break, the mailbox wouldn't come unfastened, and Shunk wouldn't stop jumping, but then, all of the sudden, in a miraculous turn of events, Shunk's stuck gears shook loose and he actually started running down the road like a greyhound on the rabbit in a legitimate full out gallop, the mailbox dead on his tail, dragging right along, throwing out a shower of sparks off the pavement, but now no longer snapping, because Shunk had hammered his wicked mouth shut so tight it couldn't open and flattened the monster's head as flat as a hub cap, of course, with my check still somewhere inside.

Finally, while in a full run, he took one last leap so high I had to duck not to hit my head on the moon and the mailbox and post swung dangerously close flying high over both our heads, catching on a "no passing sign", the rope swinging around it to rest like a cannon ball on a chain after a couple of turns. People were honking and yelling, and though Shunk seemed to be tangled in the rope he succeeded in stomping so hard that the saddle tie that held the rope finally burst and we came loose; the mail box hanging dead in the air from the sign, swinging back and forth like a clock pendulum and the rope dropped, frizzed-up, unmoving on the ground. Finally free, Shunk kept bucking in a circle, snorting and grunting in victory for a full five minutes more.

Then, finally the storm was over.

I was still on and the mailbox was finally dead.

By the time Shunk was steady enough for me to climb down we were both a little shaky from the battle. It seemed like we'd been bucking, kicking, rearing, and running and dodging mailboxes for at least a week, but I'm sure from start to finish it hadn't been twenty minutes.

After cutting that infernal, deflated mailbox from the rope, I led Shunk the mile back home on foot, past all the cars and trucks parked along that mountain road. People started clapping, cheering, honking their horns in honor of the horse who had bravely fought and defeated the mailbox dragon, a horse who now knew how to go forward, led by his determined and idiotic rider with that infernal dead steel mailbox, now as flat as a cookie sheet, tucked under his arm, still hoping to retrieve the mail.

It would take me a full day with a hacksaw, a chain cutter, a blacksmith's hammer, and a cold chisel to finally extract my check, a little crumpled, from inside that dragon's collapsed, steel hull. There were always those days when getting the mail was just a little more involved than usual.

Some people who saw it were convinced our mailbox drama was entirely staged! That it was some kind of intricate, quasi-choreographed, action scene done with a "trained" horse and a stunt rider for one of those movies always being filmed in New Mexico by an invisible camera crew hidden somewhere in the woods.

Others more close to home attributed it all to my serious, well-attested ego problem which caused me to continue carelessly risking my life riding dangerous, unbroken horses down the highway just for the attention I'd glean.

But for most, they just enjoyed it as one of life's big, humorous amazements and took it all in stride, not even charging me for their headlight repairs.

But in the crowd and traffic there had been one lady who'd seen the entire thing and was deeply fascinated. She sensed the mystery and mythologic reality being lived out in what she'd witnessed. She wept in worry for both of us when we almost bit the pavement a couple of times. She could feel the crazed, big-hearted nobility of the horse who never once pitched to get me off, but to save both of us from disaster. She wept and laughed for the courage and skilled determination of both horse and rider to finish out such a beautiful display of riding and folly, and in an unexpected reaction to that humorous and harrowing escapade, that gentle woman fell head over heels in love with Ta Shunk and didn't think she could survive another day without him very near.

And to that end, she visited us every day for a week, loaded down with gifts and friendly praise just so she could hug Shunk and stare at her hero over the corral rails for a while.

Maybe forty years old, with big stacked up hair, big sparkly make-up, long sparkly nails, and big glued on eyelashes that opened and closed like moth wings with every word she spoke, she turned out to be one of those rare, irresistible Texans who refused to let you hate them, melting all your absurd, cradle-learned, anti-Texan prejudices by the elegant way she spoke, with the very stereotyped phrases you were taught to despise.

Both Shunk and I, still stiff and swollen as a couple of bucket-soaked ax handles and as bruised as a bushel of trampled apples from so much bucking and banging about, received this sweet, intelligent woman with as much grace as we could manage, neither of us as good a company as either of us might have wanted.

After a week of so many "y'alls," and "lil o'daddys," "idn he jess the mos handsome lilo fella?" and "I jus caint git nuf a heeam," I had already started to soften up, but when she started discussing horses in the stars, horses in Hungary, horses in the pre-gringo Texas panhandle, and her ancestors who were both Comanches and Germans, all horse people, and on and on until she had me completely charmed into selling her Ta Shunk for a very good price. Shunk would always be a rough ride, but he loved that woman, and became mostly a pasture pet, down on her place along the Pecos river only some eighteen miles away from our camp.

He spent most of his days in the shade of a beautiful and rare, large oak tree in the company of a Sardinian donkey, five Angora goats, and a big sheepdog.

Belinda's gardener and lover, Basilio, a man from Sinaloa, Mexico, was a very good rider and took Shunk strutting along the road once in a while and then every year rode him in the Santa Fe parade, where Shunk's irritating strut made him look flashier than any horse ever would. He actually won awards every year.

Shunk never again had any trouble with mailboxes, for after his famous fight, all the mailboxes heard about the outcome, and whenever Ta Shunk and his rider came upon any mailboxes, he arrogantly ignored their evil, low-life stares and just strutted past, while all the mailboxes recognizing their "better", kept their mouths shut and bowed their heads, highly relieved when he finally rode out of sight.

Chapter 13

Down a Forgotten Alley

While on a Santa Fe visit standing half asleep in line to pay for oats and salt at Romero's, the image of a short, blue-eyed stallion staring out at me from a photo on a flier pinned to the timber upright that served as the feed store corkboard startled me from my stupor. It sent a rush to my ever active head, who dropping everything he was thinking, started clawing madly through miles and miles of old layers of memories, through half-conscious recollections of life's heartbreaks and confusions, pushing through that amalgam of adolescent schemes, childhood smells, and crazy moments that sit dusty in the backroom of our minds. Jostling all my early memories, my mind was like a little kid, bottom up and grunting, bent over a five gallon bucket full of marbles digging for a long neglected but highly regarded shooter buried somewhere way down, hidden at the bottom under all the rest, his fat little fist painfully punching its way past the noisy clicking mass, fishing out recollections one by one till close to the bottom he found what he was searching for, and when he did: I finally remembered!

And there they were: the memory and the horse.

I'd known this horse from a magic time in my early adolescence, on the wilder deeper part of the Reservation; or better said, like certain others, I had often seen him at a great distance. For you couldn't actually *know* him unless you were one of his, for he was extremely wild, in charge, godlike, always far away on a hill or cliff guarding his wild band of multicolored wives and their foals grazing in the swales below. He was part of one of those many vast, inner-places of sacred landscape on the Pueblo Reservation where no white men were allowed, or could have found, where no photos could be taken, where hardly any Natives ventured and even only certain Native priests were allowed to visit as special envoys. I never saw him below me in a wash or on level ground, but only above me off in the cliffs. Always like an abalone shell glittering from the dust in the sun or bright like snow on a sunny day, shining, elusive, there, then gone when he smelled you, with his family bolting miles away in their dust.

So, illicitly, I had many times seen that stallion from a place where even Indians rarely went, from a place where even now I only brought to consciousness reluctantly, for in me, all that was forbidden land in my own soul, from a memory place inside me that I hardly ever visited any more to avoid the miles of nostalgic pain over the loss of the exquisite beauty and magic of those days; and yet how could it be, that here he was just casually staring at me again, closer than before, and twenty-five years later, from a white man's poster in a feed store advertised for breeding, only fifty miles away from his magic home, captured and presented like any other backyard horse, just standing there to do somebody's bidding?

But there he was staring back at me from a poster on a post with those same pale eyes, standing on those same thick cannon bones, a short, painted horse, sturdy and rooted to both the rocks and the wind, the same imperious stance, the same unflinching straight-through-you stare, the same heavy neck, the same six inch thick strawberry mane that hung high before it folded to the left, then like a wide waterfall of hair tumbled half the way to his knees, his tail no different, but this time almost brushing behind him on the ground.

Like an elegant horse of white quartz covered in large rambling spots of pink lichen that bent around his hind quarters, parts of his wide-sprung ribs, his narrow chest, over one hock, both ears golden red and one red eye-patch, the skin of his lips were even spotted pink and white, corrugated with deep wrinkles just like a rhino.

All his children had been rhino-lipped just like him.

When I had returned from the tropics, I hadn't gone to really look, to see if he or his herd were still there, because of course I knew in my gut that all those special horses I'd known in my youth, just like my youth and the Native world that had held both, were not to be looked for, for all of it had either evaporated in the hot, meaningless stare of modernity or tribally redefined and "fenced off", literally and psychologically, from the outside world. No matter which, I could never return and the horses themselves were rejected as colonial relics by a new generation of Natives.

But before that, days were different and the "Poster Horse" was the very type of horse we had all been riding as we grew up, *coursing* in freedom to the Canyon Wren. One hundred years previous they were the only type of horse to be found anywhere in New Mexico, not just on reservations. Everywhere.

Most of the west had already lost their versions of this same horse by the time I was born. But on the Native land upon which I grew and became a person, these powerful, short, rhino-lipped horses, of every color of stone and corn had been the only horses, there were no others.

I hadn't *really* forgotten them at all, but like so many other places inside the wilderness of my soul, where the memories of loss and betrayal kept themselves mixed together in a matrix with the magnificent and the bejeweled, the path of the heartbreak of my youth made me look forward, away from it, while I healed and even though I loved all the good horses I came upon, none of the horses I'd been riding since returning from the south were even remotely relatives to what I was looking at, captured in this photo on a feed store wall.

The inferiority complex of white American culture that flowed in and took over all the west still had encoded in their language a scale of lesser and greater that planned to plow in or eradicate anything for which they themselves were inadequate or to which they would have had to bow their heads in admiration if it wasn't their own idea. The little Spanish descended, landraced, privately owned Indian Ponies, the Cow Ponies of the American southwest, were actually very highly prized and admired by a lot of individual "white" people such as Thomas Jefferson, James Aubrey, Frank Dobie. But in the main, they fell prey to lesser minds manipulated by the ignorance of the "New World" order, whose fiery flood of morbid, protestant hatred for the "small, non-English-speaking, beautifully dressed and brown skinned", had singed the flamboyance and beauty off the cultures throughout the west.

Every Indian knew that the Iberian colonial's tiny horse that they received had been adopted, absorbed, replicated, and regrown in Native ground and water until they were both ecologically and spiritually landraced into their own culture; re-assembled both in physical form and spiritual matrix just like all the iron, wheat, wool, goat milk cheese, apples, peaches, plums, San Rafael, and Jesus—with whom these Barb horses arrived—all of which were re-indigified and absorbed to become treasured details in the people's bigger existence and definition of themselves. The horses, actively changed in form, function, and position, now became the vehicle for various Natively understood deified forces and therefore became legitimately and utterly the horses of these Pueblo people and re-born side-by-side with them from their own land.

The post-WWII New Mexico Indian Reservation I was raised in was exceptional, for they arduously worked at retaining their culture, dress, food, language, ceremonialism, agriculture, and horses—not by freezing it all in an image or liturgical recitation—but by navigating their tribal fate in a unique way of their own invention, whereby the core of who they are decolonized what they absorbed before they were absorbed by it, indigifying it all. They did not reject the incoming culture: they converted it to their purposes. Jesus became an Indian, iron a type of sacred flint, wheat became Jesus' corn, and horses came from the Sea and Sun—and San Esteban and San Rafael, the horse's Saints, became Native deities.

The mandatory, so-called "white", American, education system worked hard to cloud and eradicate this clear and real vision. The generation of Native youths that came just after my time in school, reacted to this pro-middle-America proselytizing by becoming even richer, more affectated, more acceptable to fancy art museums, cultural events, and all sorts of money ventures to outrun the system of the whites by being better at it than they were, all of course in hopes of maintaining their tribal self-esteem by so doing. But the whiteness in so-called "white people" was a tricky phenomena. "Whites" were a product of their own ancestor's cultural losses to the same process they now peddled and pushed onto the Natives. There was no proviso in any of that for the survival of magic Indigenous vision in anything they were teaching or living out, because they had lost their own.

The horses that had been bodily part of their Native Pueblo people, all of a sudden, one day, started looking like a colonial intrusion to the "educated" youth. Since their little horses didn't seem to impress the stigmatized, pseudo-sophistication of the "new" white settler mind, ironically the wonderful little horses got lost in the cultural sanitization. So to impress this new, shallow-minded self-designation of what it meant to be Native, in came the Arabian horses, (who the whites erroneously thought were the pure, ancestral horses from which the original Rez horses descended). In came the Thoroughbreds, the Halflingers, and of course the ubiquitous Quarter Horse, who flooded out even the American Stock Horse among the cowboys, whose original ranks had quite a bit of Spanish/Indian/Cow Pony gracing them as well. But that finished that.

The popular assumption that all the horses Native people owned they obtained from wild herds is no more than a simple-minded attempt by the ruling culture to diminish the expertise that Natives had with stock raising before "Americanism". While it's true that a lot of Indian horses went wild after the tribes were concentrated, exterminated, or forced to abandon them sometimes becoming large wild herds, most of these were captured and slaughtered for army meat in WWI and WWII and then for pet food in the 1950's.

All the original horses of the Natives who were corralled onto reservations, had always been raised in private herds of family-bred horses for centuries. The horses Natives rode were these, not the remnants of white people's imagined feral herds, as every book pretends to teach. Miraculously, we as kids were riding the last of these marvelous animals, but with no knowledge that they were any different, never thinking they would ever diminish, and never ever thinking of them as a "breed": the eternal definition that civilization's people need in order to legitimize the worth of any living organism, including humans.

Civilizations develop "breed" standards and societies ostensibly to save breeds of animals and plants. But without the original human life style, corresponding culture, function, and land that must go with these animals, all horses, like grapes, grain, and people morph into the form of whatever is trying to save them. Wine grapes from Bordeaux, France grown in Tennessee don't make Bordeaux wine. They make Tennessee wine, but not Bordeaux. It's not just the genetics. These breed designations only serve to freeze a limited aspect of a type, which ends up entropically destroying the original because it doesn't include the bigger picture of what landraced the animal to begin with. Strangely most horse breeds are just frozen and legislated human opinions about horses. The horses, if real, should define themselves. But this would necessitate a people who owned them to have a lifestyle that corresponded to the horse's original situation. No lawns, no cities, no fences, no satellites.

But there he was: at least one of the most famous herd stallions of my very own youth, presumed extinct or his bloodline absorbed, gone, an image of a virtual God, captured at someone's house, a horse whose territory had been sacred and *never* photographed staring back at me off a flimsy feed store poster, with a phone number attached whereby one could simply make an appointment to see this supernatural horse and breed your Quarter Horse mare to him!

It was very strange and bordering on the obscene to me and I had no idea what was going on. But, I was definitely going to call! Not only because this horse was who he was and I wanted to find out how it happened that some non-Indian just *had* him, but also because this horse had to be very up in years. He was already old when I was twelve years old and if this old fellow was still making babies he would have to be between forty and fifty years old! Possible, but not likely. A mystery lay inside it all. It was like calling up a real estate dealer in southern New Mexico and asking for an appointment to see Victorio, who they claim they had out back in a cage! It was really that pronounced and obnoxious to me.

This was all a spin in my head and in that reverie I hadn't noticed how stationery I'd become in the cash register line and was holding up traffic, whose cue was getting longer and longer with people patiently waiting to pay for their doggy toys, baby chicks, feed store hay, cinches, birdseed, kitty litter, and straw. But this was quickly solved by a man and woman, recently arrived from some other zone of middle America, who hadn't quite adjusted to the more gradual, personal character of life in northern New Mexico, who, unceremoniously, just elbowed their way to the front of the line, pushing me to the side like an old chair, the rest following like a school of little fish, until I was last.

We didn't have any phones at our camp and as big Tom Romero, the store owner's nephew, who was running the register that day was a long time acquaintance, I thought to ask him if I could use the company phone to contact the people claiming to own this Abalone-colored horse.

I could wait. The pushy couple up at the register, now paying for their small bag of fancy, "little-dog" dog food, apparently didn't like the way I looked or my very presence in the feed store and were running a prickly, ranting diatribe at a New York decibel level, knocking my clothing style, running down my silk neck scarves, sterling slide, my painted, smoke-tanned, elk-skin duster, my silver buttoned botas with beaded knee garters, my hand woven knee-length shirt, my piled silver bracelets, silver belt, and even my fancy hat and silver hatband, my hair, and everything else, especially, of course, my belt knife. Luckily I hadn't spoken to them or they would've freaked out for my reservation accent. Everything about me was "wrong".

But Tom was accustomed to all types and just continued ringing them up. Then the man pointing at me behind my back asked:

"I'm surprised you people let guys like that just roam around loose! Aren't you afraid he might try something?"

Always courteous, Tom handed the fellow his bill, and smiling, asked "Where are you folks from?"

"We just moved here from Indiana."

"You don't have people like him where you're from?"

"Oh, Good Lord, I should say not, they'd lock up a nut like that on the spot."

"And you came *here* to live? Too bad. Because this place is full of people like him. He's actually a born and bred local."

Then the lady started chirping again.

"Well, I would sure hate to run into him in some dark alley!"

Twenty-eight-year-old Tom, all six and a half feet of him, always a gentleman, but strong enough to lift a sixty-five pound bale of hay in each hand and toss them simultaneously up a stack six layers high like a couple of cereal boxes—in normal northern New Mexico etiquette—stared sweetly at the man while addressing the lady...

"Pardon me, Ma'am, but you've got this guy all wrong. That man there is a good man and a highly respected medicine man; his mother was a Native and he's a horseman from Hell. I'm sure none of us will ever know all there's to know about him, but what I do know, is this: we don't have too many dangerous, dark alleys here, but if you or your husband ever find a dark, dangerous alley you're afraid to go down, that man there would be the man you'd want along with you to keep you safe."

The crowd laughed, one of the old matrons at the end of the line poked me in the ribs. I jumped and laughed, the people paid, Tom grinned, and then yelled to the back of the line.

"Martín, you folks busy out there? Heard about your mailbox-killing horse, you still got 'em?"

"Why? Did you want to buy 'em? Nah, I sold him to a nice Texas lady." I yelled back.

When the couple from Indiana heard my accent their heads spun round toward me staring in utter terror. Departing with their little dog, dog food bags clutched under their arms like footballs and with scared, evil looks on their faces they stomped past me and out of the store mumbling under their breath: "I sometimes think New Mexicans just don't know they're supposed to be part of our United States."

Hearing my voice, Vera, Tom's auntie emerged from the back room and yelled to me in her more southern Colorado accent: "Hey Martín, did you hear what happened to Tom's sheep?"

"Did something happen to your sheep?"

"Aliens, man, almost got my sheep."

"Aliens? What aliens?"

"From outer space, aliens."

"They got your sheep?"

"No, No, almost, my sheep were due to lamb and then one night they all just ran away heading west out of Amalia, I followed them on Rojito, off there in the middle of nowhere over on those sage flats, you know where I mean, toward the river where the aliens had their landing place."

"They had a landing place?"

"Yeah. Big upright pillars in a big circle with all kinds of crazy stuff hanging off them. The ewes had already all dropped twin lambs there. The grass was huge next to the pillars, right in the middle of the snow, from the heat of their spaceships."

"Did you see the aliens?"

"No, but they were coming, I know it. I think I got there just in time. They must've telepathically called my sheep to the landing spot. It took me two days to get all my animals back to Amalia, there were at least fifty mamas with two babies each."

"Boy, I'm glad you got all your sheep back."

I guess those people were right about New Mexico.

Chapter 14

The Abalone Horse

Seeing that poster signaled the close of my short-lived, semi-successful career as a buyer of unwanted, backyard horses, during which time I had joyfully attempted to summon all their natural grandeur into a tangible usefulness through the intense, mental concentration and forward effort necessary to pick our way, together, up and over the rough terrain and altitudes of our mountain trails and byways; afterwards selling them proud, capable, and tuned up to other people who held them in equally high esteem. Though I bought a lot of horses after that, except for one, I never again took a horse home with any intention to sell. I actually started giving good horses as gifts to those I felt deeply loved having them.

With more intensity and some old abandon that reappeared from my reservation-reared soul, I began to ride farther and harder than ever, but no longer on the backs of any backyard Quarter Horse crosses like Juniper or any grade marvels like Shindai. This was not for any other reason than the fact that horses descended from those that I had given up for lost from my early days began miraculously drifting back into my daily existence.

Though I didn't know it yet, in a way mostly unjust but totally ironic, what little remained of the descendants of these worthy Spanish and Native horses were now being "preserved" by white people for white people, jealously held inside the rigid grip of the descendants of the same people whose mentality of hatred for Indians, Spanish speaking locals, and their "little" horses had caused the virtual disappearance of those beautiful little horses from the American west to begin with!

It would have been different if these "modern settlers" had understood and owned up to the grief and reality of their part in that history, then they would've been heroes to us all.

But unlike the Native and Spanish descended ranching families, who by the fashion they lived in the land they lived on—cultures who helped landrace these creatures into the amazing southwestern horse they became—these modern, machine-dependent "settlers" of the late twentieth century had no intention or awareness of giving these horses any tangible Indigenous cultural ground upon which to thrive or recognition that their tremendous beauty and value didn't come from genetic preservation. You could not just "breed for" what these horses had become. The more older, conducive lifestyle—with its long transportation distances, wide open spaces, old time tack, method of riding, and usefulness in the people's daily work and ritual life—from which these horse's physical and athletic substance descended had to be there. Instead these "new type of people" have always felt they were a "superior consciousness" who were going to "fix" the horse's "faults" by breeding them to fit a standard for horses that had already ruined any number of other culturally landraced horses worldwide. A standard that had been determined and laid down for Thoroughbreds, etc. by wealthy, out-of-touch elitists.

That day at the feed store, Tom and Vera had pulled the phone out of my reach and tried to warn me:

"No, I won't let you use the phone, Martín, not to call the number on that poster. That scene over there is a can of worms, maddog infighting, a ball of haywire all crazy, whoa, let me tell you, you don't want to get your foot stuck in that mess!" Tom laughed, still holding the phone just beyond my grasp.

"They've got piles of horses like that one in the poster, but of every color. They have all those old time ones, you know, like my mothers' fathers always had. The same ones everybody used to have: from every Reservation, from old Spanish families, from old settlers, and even cowboy families. Some little, old-time surveyor from up north somewhere started gathering up as many of these old time horses as he could find and eventually got talked into making him a club to keep these fine little horses from being bred out of existence. But like all registries, the members, who were too distant from those of us who had the horses originally, became experts and fought over details about which horse was really an old time horse or not. Ridiculous. Then with too much whiskey, they all broke up, each party running off with their horses and restarting four new drinking clubs. Then they all fought again. It's all a mess. There's only a few of those real Indian horses or Cow Pony *Mesta* descended horses left in the country and now, 'cause of these people, they're all over the place, in backyards and little pens, in the hands of these crazy people who want them to be everything except what they are and fight over what that's supposed to be. If you've gotta go there to look at the horses of this particular group of owners, Don't Call! If it were me, I wouldn't even let them know I was coming." Plopping a feed catalog on the counter, Tom started to draw out a map on the back with a pen.

"Look, I'll tell you how to get there, then just go on over. Drive past first just to check it out and if you're lucky none of those people will be there. If nobody's there, just drive on in, nobody will say anything, people are always coming and going. Then go ahead and take a look, get it all out of your system, then get going! I know how you feel. But really, friend, don't get tangled up with that stuff over there, I know more than I'm telling. Best just to let it go like all the rest. The past is past, it's a terrible loss but we just have to accept it."

But of course, I didn't. I knew perfectly well how things always change, but I didn't accept having to lose a lot of good just because they were from an age no longer understood, any more than we should retain an ugly destructive modus operandi from the present just because it was familiar.

Only three miles straight down the road from the store and still in the city limits, on an incongruous, still grassy strip of original south Santa Fe prairie, wedged between a cement plant and an affordable housing project, a row of heavy duty pens filled with horses ran out exactly where and how Tom had described.

No humans appeared to be around, so I rolled my Ford slowly around the corner and drove on in. After turning off the engine, I let my old truck coast to a quiet stop beside an impressive, two and a half story tall hay shed roofed over with recycled tin and shored up, like all the pens, with railroad ties and recycled rubber stripping from some industry's discarded conveyor belting.

I waited, New Mexico style, for the ever present dogs that always guard every ranchito to commence their usual bark-and-snarl alarm. But, strangely, there was no barking. Instead a very friendly, waggy-tailed, little heeler-collie appeared and lay down in front of the pen to my right which, to my great surprise, housed the very horse whose photo had graced the feed store poster. When no humans showed up, I stepped out of the truck and went to say hello to that beautiful, wild-looking horse.

The hay in the barn was really bad and rotten, smelling very strongly of mildew and was probably heating up. That penetrating unhealthy stink, combined with the creosote fumes of the ties and the rubber of the pens, attacked one's olfactory senses. But still it's oppressive presence failed to overpower the wondrous, sweet, warm aroma of over sixty of those rare, earth-descended horses milling in their rubber cages.

They were all of the type we had known so well. I really was amazed. Of course, they were not the actual horses I'd known, not the individuals anyway, but they were still definitely the same kind and maybe some of their direct descendants.

Any of us from the village of my youth would have known them anywhere. But now, standing face to face with this poster stallion, himself planted in his impound, without the cliffs and dust and cobble of home, it was also clear that he wasn't actually the same horse I had earlier supposed him to be. He was an actor. He looked like the original, at least he was wearing his suit and stood just like him. But he was just the image of what turned out to be his grandfather, for the original fire and mystique were obviously missing; but he really did look the part.

There were horses everywhere and for the most part they were my kind of horse. All except for two mares, one very old red one, who roaming free started eating the paint off my truck hood and an apple bottomed, liver bay who seemed pregnant, both of them out of a different sack of beans than all the rest.

My mind instinctively registered the individual timbres of all the whinnies of foals, the snorts of mares, and their snuffling, one wheeze, a squeal, and the grunts of mane-tossing-face-fighting stud colts who were rearing up, barely into view above the smelly, obnoxious, stringy, spiderwebs of rubber. The symphony of the varied sounds that different individual horses make always magically correspond to the symphony of their varied colors and markings.

The long line of rubber-belted pens reminded me of the first time, as a child, I'd been allowed to accompany some Pueblo parents of my childhood friends to the town of Berna-lillo to buy sea shells. Then only a main street, with two stores facing each other from opposite sides of the unpaved road, the entire town was owned by one of two warring extended families: the Silvas and the Montoyas, each of whom owned an entire side; the Montoyas to the east; the Silvas to the west!

Pueblo Natives from different villages came to Silva's store to purchase sea shells as raw material to break, grind, and drill into the heishi, shell bead necklaces for which our village was world famous. Sometimes it seemed as if every man and woman and child in the village over six, who wasn't busy farming or tending ritual, was busy hand-drilling shell beads with a pump drill. Even I drilled beads. The experts drilled turquoise stone beads and coral beads as well. Tribal members had plenty of sources for sea shells and even more for stones from a myriad of well established providers, many of whom were familiar and colorful, itinerant Anglo traders and traders from Mexico, who could be counted on to wander through the villages in seasonal cycles like migratory birds. But when a family ran low on bead material between their visits, a representative would make the trip in the back of someone's pickup truck to Silvas' store, on the west side of the road in Bernalillo.

Though a thousand miles away from the nearest ocean shore, every time the door to that store opened, a delightful smell just like the sea: lusty, a little rank, and sweet wafted onto the street. For inside, running the entire sixty foot of it's width, a wall of sixty angular wooden bins, back to back, four foot high and two foot across were filled to brimming with tons of different types of shells from all the seas of the world.

Every one of us from this arid, sandy land that millions of years past was itself the bottom of the ocean, loved the smell of that store. Piles and piles of shells, sold wholesale only to Indians, rose up in each bin, which held a different shell type, whose colors blended in a subtlety of sunsets or stretches of warm seas, some white to purple, others orange to tinted salmon, some with translucent aragonite layers over greens and blues, others with bright blue lips and brown inner layers and some just light purple to dark purple to black purple, every permutation of every color, and four bins of plain white clams, the most popular.

All the world's people descend from what must've been an amazing prehistoric phenomena, in the period after the Ice Ages, when we lived almost exclusively on shellfish and often right on top of shell midden mounds right along the inlets and the sea. Because all the horses came from the sea, Natives understood horse colors like the shells of those beasts who are born from, live in, and die with the Mother sea. To them, the horses still have the colors of their ancestral, mythologic ocean forbears: the shellfish!

Everybody knew that mountain bluebirds got their color from the blue canyon mists of springtime made into holographic feathers and that white corn comes from the finger nails of the Holy Mothers of Life whose nails are opals, which are understood to be dawn light captured inside petrified water, all of which in turn comes from the white aragonite layer of ocean clam shell. This was a Native alchemy that everybody knew and that was held alive in the way Indigenous languages are spoken. To white people it was all just poetry and metaphor, but to Indians this was the tangible substance of their Gods.

The horses of their old Native culture were considered to have been generated from the same Mother-force as all the Indians themselves. While the substance of their horses were built from the wild grasses and the agates of cliffs, the winds of the plains, all the mountains and the surf, their horses inherited their vast array of coat colors from the substance of corn, corn whose body is the body of the Goddess and also the body of all the people. Corn whose colors are in turn born from Her as the Sea. Made from the substance of the Ocean's vast array of sea shells: the finger nails of our Mother of Life, they are the same sea shells upon which Native corn growers, for over three millennia, throughout the Americas and Caribbean depended on in order to release the rich nutrients of their corn. By burning the same shells of Her sea into shell lime and with which they in turn boiled their maize, they created the ubiquitous nixtamal, as their daily bread, whose substance in turn became the bodies of the actual human species to the Native, ritual mind throughout the continent.

Corn and horses and shells. Corn, people, shells. People, corn, and horses were not intertwined, but all fruit off the same vine, from the same Mother.

So in every bin in Silvas, a color of the hard, bejeweled, biomineral husk of a soft little sea animal lay, captured and mounded up. Shells made by the unlikely magic of those little animals ability to lick their own gorgeous houses into view around them with their tongue-like mantels, by which means they produce designs and colors for which, after years of scientific study, no bioscience has been capable of accurately ascribing a practical function or any scientific reason for existing.

These flamboyant shapes and colors do nothing to attract a mate, because of course their mate just sits in the sea bottom silt and waits for the free floating seeds. Plus, shellfish, though many do have eyes, do not see the color of the inside of their neighbor's shell, much less the beautiful inside of their own creations while alive. They are seen by no one until the artist has died and left all those colors behind in hard bio-mineral!

What also surprises researchers is that the millions of colors of the vast races and species of mollusks worldwide all make their colors with hormones produced by the animal, which in human bodies regulate reproduction, immune response, and general life changes; but in mollusks these hormones become mineral color producers. The designs they make have no detectable protestant or rationalist evolutionary species survival function. But as attested by the fossil record, these ever-evolving, wild forms that shells have created, have been for hundreds of millions of years, dedicated to pushing the envelope of imagination into reality of a vast variety of beauty in the form of shells. A beauty upon which reproduction or food getting does not rely! To the contrary: mollusks reproduce and strain food from the sea in order to live, just to make more and more beautiful shells! This motive of living to make beauty is what Natives themselves participate in by proudly creating exquisite shell bead necklaces that they wear around their necks. The scientists who are cool, love this, the rest are unscientific, because since their civilization biased minds can't find a way to test it to the contrary, they refuse to accept hundreds of experiments that indicate mollusks make their beautiful patterns and colors only because they do and must. The natural world is dedicated to beauty.

Horse's colors work along the same lines: they are vast and beautiful. Like the colors of Native corn and seashells, they are not limited to the tight compartments of white, black, brown, red, yellow, and blue. They come in mind-boggling combinations. The permutations of horse's reflective and refractive coat colors in the sun are infinite. Endless patterns and markings with wild nuances of over two hundred shades and patterns of horse coat colors in endless combinations are the treasured subject matter of a large body of ancient, orally-preserved, mythic literature among all ancient horse raising people, especially the nomadic ancestors of many European cultures, North and West Africans, Native Americans, and the older manifestation of the American Cowboy. They all understood and designated a myriad of beautiful and metaphorically ornate color descriptions for these old time horses. What has happened to people today? Could it be they can't see those colors any more? I often wonder what else in their beautiful world people today might not be seeing, when looking point blank at a red pointed, steel blue grulla with black striped ears, smokey withers, hash marked forelegs, three color striped agate hooves, a golden sun fade and dapples, black mane and tail they ask, "Oh isn't that horse just gray?" They must live in a world where the rain is gray and the sun yellow! Depressing.

Even science says the variety of horse colors are vast, but nonetheless there are colors and patterns they haven't quite comprehended just yet, patterns that some horses produce and others cannot that are not simply genetically obtained. Like seashells, something else is at work!

Pueblo old timers, some Spanish speakers, and Navajos call their corn and their horses by the same names as the colors of seashells. In just the way that myriad types of shellfish worldwide, after being dredged up from the sea or after washing up on the shores having lived out their artistic lives and their outer husks are gathered together and poured into bins, separated by type and color, in places like Silva's, so that even thousands of miles away from their home, sea, and beach, their colors and shapes could still enchant us, their smells still causing our hearts to sail the freedom of the surf—with just that same magic—these many rows of pens with old style horses, of every wild natural horse color we'd ever known, had a smell and look that took me to other ages, places, and times in my life.

Horses once numbering in the millions—whose fine and formerly, high-held position among the original Natives and early settling Spanish speakers and even a few early exploring east coasters and white cowboy admirers—had been unjustly sifted out of the modern settler consciousness, but in whose wild colors today, one could still distinguish these Barb pony's colors as not only freedom and territory lost, but the color and smell of what it meant to be truly at home in a land as wild and beautiful as New Mexico.

West of the Mississippi and north of the Missouri, certain registries have now adopted some northern Plains Indian names for horse colors. Various nomadic Native horse cultures of the central buffalo-plains called horses bearing the colors of this poster horse a red roan "medicine hat" for the similarity in appearance to that of a Red Buffalo Horn Headdress worn by the priests of certain mystic societies of both men and women.

But where I grew up, in the southwest, certain Native cultures called such a horse an Abalone Horse: a horse with the fabulous, holographic, aragonite shimmer of the inside of a red abalone shell written all over his body. And everyone knew that Abalone Horses were often born with blue eyes. So, blue-eyed Abalone Horses are said to have a body made of abalone, eyes made of turquoise, with lips made of spotty, purple olivella shell. This type of horse was the specific type of Holy horse that carried the Sun Father powerfully puffing across the big high desert skies, lending his bright reflective iridescent coat to the horizon in one of those famous abalone sunsets for which our territory is well known. For Natives, the painted colors of these horses were not a sign of "mixed blood" betraying some "cold blooded" ancestry, as some ignorant, race-insistent sections of the Euro-Americans supposed in the past. Abalone Horses were the evidence of differing powers in the Earth and Ocean where red ochre cliffs and sea foam bred together to became an abalone roan. These horses had been handed over to the Mother of Life to distribute at her discretion to various tribal people and Gods whom she felt deserved them and who could understand their spiritual royalty. The Sun himself received the blue-eyed Abalone Paint for his ride from his own mother.

Just as the villagers to whom these horses used to belong didn't wear shell *colored* necklaces, or eat shell *colored* corn, or own shell *colored* horses, they wore necklaces made of real polished shell and real stone, ate corn whose substance they knew to be biologically shell descended and they rode and raised horses whose substance were *made* of shell, turquoise, corn, and wind: jeweled horses that always knew how to bring us home. The jeweled shell necklace made of drilled shell discs was what all southwestern Natives traded for their mane-flying, shimmering, and shiny coated horses. Up until 1950, one drilled, heishi, shell-bead necklace could buy one horse. The two things were originally the same thing in people's mind.

And there, that day, these fabulous but dejected gathered animals stood in the magnificence of all their gathered colors, organized into official categories like shells in wooden bins, waiting in ugly pens, for the confused desires of boring, modern, polyester-wearing, settler people to dish them out to people just like them, who would agree to preserve the horses the way the "owners" dictated. But none of this Indigenous horse color magic seemed to be able to paint it's complexity into their hearts. Its majesty should've healed the settler's unhappy souls. But even if all of the knowledge and mystique could've been accepted as valid, it would never be truly embraced as anything but an interesting "relic of the past", for it would imply that pretty much everything these "new settlers" believed in would have to be dropped and something more original learned, especially their unquestioned superiority and the illusion of their so-called progress out of an ignorant past.

But somewhere barely conscious inside these "settlers" of modern times, they must've felt the presence of the grandeur of something they wanted, but sadly couldn't seem to get their minds around, or they wouldn't have instinctively tried to "preserve" such horses. But the methods they held to were destructive to their proclaimed cause. As absurd as a people who would invade a country with armed troops just to drink coffee with the locals in a café, in order to experience the way of life and land they were destroying by the very motive of their presence, they searched for ways to best "preserve" their horses by forcing them into a limiting genetic breed standard that only served to atrophy and dwindle further what they pretended to "preserve".

Then of course, they argued about how to "save" the horses.

Some said making feral herds was the answer. But letting them go feral would give the horses nothing.

It was then decided that training them all into acceptable arena horses high stepping around with painted hooves, shaved off whiskers, and pulled tails in aimless show-horse military maneuvers was the best way to get people to buy them. Thinking that competitive commerce would somehow preserve "the breed". This was all a waste of the horses immense wonder and an insult to their original substance.

The secret that all horse registries seem to ignore is that the physical presence of these horses was only one third of the reality of their actual existence; a complete horse could not live only in a horse's genetics or performance capacity for spectators. All types of horses were originally parts of a lifestyle without which they cease being those types of horses. The horse itself was only one third of the "horse". The second third of their beings lived in the souls of the original peoples into whose lives and ritual existence they had matrixed. The last third was where, for hundreds or even thousands of years, the horse's people and the people's horses both equally needed the very land and the open air lifestyle that the land had always demanded and held them both. Thus the people's lifestyle, the physical horses, and the land all had to be there for the three parts to function together, causing the horses to be complete beings, causing the people to be complete horse people and the land to welcome them both completely!

The desire and possibility of all this was, of course, still sitting right there underneath all these horse's skins. You could feel it. You could even see it percolating, thundering in hope, and waiting to burst back into life again. Behind that ugly rubber they still dreamed of that three-way wholeness, not unlike a lot of other animals and people so distanced from their land and souls.

You couldn't just "breed" color horses, teach them to jump walls, do horse shows, and claim you'd saved the horse. By the time this happened, these Native/Spanish horses would be as limited and removed from their own selves as the rest of civilization's animals and people. All of this smelled the same as what happened when Native Americans were pushed into boarding schools. No doubt the people doing all this felt they themselves were being saved by "saving" a horse breed, just like Christian missionaries felt they were being saved by saving Natives from their "backwards Native ways". But like Native American people, these horses were not some simple genetic uniqueness, they were the blossoms of a culture and lifestyle that white people had come to despise because it made their own limited, repressed lifestyle feel strangely inadequate. They had even extirpated any of their own "whites" in the past who had loved the wild and could live like their horses wanted. There had been so-called "whites" who had been able to understand and live that way, but the "settler culture" itself would not allow even them to co-exist, for settler culture was by definition made mostly of immigrants already cruelly haunted by a spiritually flattened past and trivialized before they ever got here. They came from a flattened European world that had flattened their pasts and their minds until it was familiar. Ironically, they needed the world of their second chance to remain flattened because it was all they knew and they misconstrued their own reality by thinking that they somehow were no longer flattened if they were now the "Flatteners" in control of colonially flattening the Natural and the Native world. So they wanted the land cleared of Big Living little people and their little horses. Settlers were constantly neutering their own futures by writing the real Native soul out of the land they overran, in the end, driving off the vitality of the land that could have given them life as well.

But even so, not everything had been conquered, it was not all finished; for on that day, staring back at me, with three generations of eyes behind their own, these horses were still here, still going, still hoping, still waiting, and I was there to see them seeing me.

These thoughts were zooming around in me like iridescent swallows pouring out from under a highway bridge, while I inhaled into my soul the delight of all those old time horse's smell over again—for not having smelled it for years, they were a very different smell than a Quarter, Arab, or a Trakehner—when someone tiptoed up on me and touched me on my buckskinned arm. I jumped and spun and almost succeeded in knocking down a sturdy young white woman trying to smile, but more startled than I was, who politely asked in a very smooth, upper class British accent:

"Very sorry to startle you, sir, but can I help you? Are you looking for the owners, perhaps?"

Chapter 15
Zajlani

The original Abalone Horse, the stallion of the cliffs and many painted mares, the one I'd known from those more magic, far away times on forbidden ground, from the dust and cobbles of my youth was not the horse that stared back at me from the poster, but the grandfather of the poster horse.

But the poster horse did have a famous father, the foal of the original Abalone Horse, who had come from my homeland. The father was still alive, hauled off somewhere, also an Abalone Horse, being fought over by whites and known to them by at least three different names depending on which club they defended, but his whereabouts was always a cloak and dagger affair.

This son of the three-named stallion was only one of eight foals: three boys and five girls dropped into life from a little red wild Barb mare in those dramatic canyons west of Valencia, New Mexico. She was a descendant of a Navajo herd who'd been hidden north of Ladron Peak, when the Diné were cruelly hauled off to the concentration camp in 1863 at Fort Sumner.

The poster horse had all the look of his grandpa but had none of his punch, for of course he'd grown up as the "poster horse", trying to save Indian horses from their Indianness and he didn't grow up on the Rez, he was a city boy like his long line of owners.

But he was undeniably a beautiful horse nonetheless.

Annie, the English girl who'd startled me, cleaned these ferocious looking stalls and stacked manure in exchange for part of the purchase price of a well built dun gelding; one of these beautiful Barb horses, as she was calling them now, a horse who at first glance, could have been, at least in looks, the very twin of my best friend's famous *gallo* horse as a kid way back on the Reservation.

The liturgy of stories and attempted pedigrees of every one of these beautiful beasts and their former owners was extolled to me, like an indoctrination spiel, as together we strolled from pen to pen down the rows of dark banded pens.

When the turgid mental muck and absurd tangle of all the infighting, machinations, and politics of rich people's horse rivalry—all in the name of horse rescue, to camouflage a tax write off—came to a density beyond the New Mexico open air's ability to clear, I felt I might have to puke.

But I gallantly listened and when it came to the individual

horses who stood there, it turned out that quite a few actually did descend from the life and land I knew in my youth, but this upper crust horse lady was not interested in anything I could add about their origins before the new "settlers" had gotten hold of them. It was as if time began only with this litany of recent white owners who all had names. Before these "owners", the horses were all just Indian horses or Spanish horses; no individuals, no Tribal names, an anonymous past!

These animals were part of my body and my history, and better people than me before me. But ownership is all modernity honors and since these "owners" felt they owned the land and the horses — no matter how cool, hip, or free thinking they could act, their infighting clan alone owned the "truth" about "their" horses, which were galvanized into the tales that modern owner families told themselves over and over and dealt out to anyone they could sell it too.

As an actual dues paying member in the registry and an equal in economic class and cultural position, Annie figured that since she knew "the story" and was now herself an actual "owner" she knew "everything" there was to know!

Never one to be discouraged, when I realized the "owners" that she "worked" for were selling her a horse, I intimated that I would love to buy that Abalone stallion who'd been peering at me from the poster, postulating that I could probably find the rest of his soul if I could just get him out of town.

Annie sneered.

"You? You couldn't handle that one, besides he's very rare, they'd never let him go!"

Like a horse, I wanted to shake my head, straighten out my mane, and shed that worthless jibe, but I stood still and undeterred, allowing the vapor of the sting and the imperial ignorance to merge with the acrid smell of bad hay until all of it drifted off and out of town on a passing dust devil. After all, I thought to myself, she was probably better than the "owners"!

Imagine, the very horses from our Native Earth and lifestyle being held off limits and away from those of us who had actually personally known the land, the people, and the grandparents of the animals by those usurpers who now claimed to own and know everything about them.

Sometimes quiet conquers. So I said nothing and stood unmoving for a long time. To break her discomfort at my well-practiced Indian silence, she finally blurted out:

"Well, if you're really interested in getting a Barb, they're selling this stallion's younger sister, but she's just a plain old roan, not so good looking, and she's totally green."

And of course...

I bought her.

● ● ●

The first six months after the poster horse's sister came to live with us, Taa Diné families from the Navajo Reservation comprised the greater percentage of the clients that I doctored. They liked to alternate locations where I did my curing and ceremonies on their behalf, generously coming to pick us up and transporting my family the three hundred miles to their family districts in *Dinétah*. A month or two later, they returned to our Northern New Mexico mountains, bringing all their relatives in caravans of a dozen trucks and Blazers.

Those were big, good doings at our place along the mountain creek, roasting goats and sheep, the old and young ladies helping Dolores at the fire, the older guys inside helping with me, their children up in the corrals with the horses.

They're the ones who finally found a name for the Abalone Horse's granddaughter.

Like most of the horses that came to grace our ever-widening camp of cabins, outbuildings, barns, corrals, and fancy painted tipis in the pines and firs, this pretty mare became friendly with all and grew into a celebrity for the families of my clients.

A beautiful strawberry roan with an orangey-red ochre dorsal stripe running from mane to tail, no spots, one white sock, a dishwater blond mane, and a long tail to match, and with a little leaf shaped white headlight on her forehead, she was a horse that really liked to talk.

Whinnying at every little change, every new bird, every person, every changing direction of the wind, every truck or car, every dog, other horses, she bugled away in all kinds of pitches and timbres, grunting and nickering loud and soft, high and low, especially if someone would play soccer with her.

She loved balls of every sort. Groaning and squealing all the while, she'd swing her foreleg forward so cleanly as to drive a soccer ball with her hoof ninety miles per hour hissing past your ears, then spring around three hundred and sixty degrees, waiting for the next pitch!

In my entire life I'd never heard any other horse with so many sounds in her belly.

During one of these ceremonial get-togethers the following fall, one of the Blackgoat family aunties started calling this mare Zajlani, or "many words". The Navajo name for a mockingbird.

It took a little while, but her name eventually stuck, but her saddle certainly didn't, at least not at first.

Zajlani's wrinkly rhino lips, like all her clan, were amazingly agile. She could work them like a tapir's trunk, like a short elephant snout which, along with her very sharp teeth, she could untie, unfasten, or unclick any buckle, knot, clip, or gate latch. She never ran off, but nothing could contain her for more than a moment.

You'd be trying to saddle and as soon as you had one girth fastened and were working on the next she'd have the other one unbuckled on the opposite side!

Eventually she accepted the saddle and my cool, old-time, softened-white-rawhide, ochre-painted head stall with a hand-forged snaffle and horse hair reins. She quickly learned to go, turn, stop, and change gaits to the point where she would let me ride: her body shaking and screaming with loud whinnies announcing every change.

Though never a race horse, she was plenty fast, fairly smooth, and had a few extra gaits. She took the long haul like a tank, with an ability to make turns so tight she could have eaten her own tail, then straight away out she'd pull up inclines as sure footed as a rock squirrel, yelling the entire way.

On the flat or straight she always rocked and leaned forward like an ice-skater, always grunting and going to get there. Like all her type, Zajlani never, ever tired.

She became my horse for longer stints and since my riding was no longer any kind of employment, I went out for greater distances, to magical places you couldn't get to in a truck.

Then one afternoon, after a three-hour-round-trip from an old ruins, just as her and I pulled into our camp, she began to dance in a way I'd never seen and because I didn't know what was coming, she catapulted me off so cleverly and unopposed that I landed square on my butt, straddling a hummock of grass and peering right into our cabin's doorway!

Like everybody knows, you can usually tell when a horse decides to buck, so when their back stiffens and that head's getting ready to drop and they start to windup for the lift-off, you pull up the head then turn it, then before they rear you get their head back down and keep countering whatever they cook up until it's settled, or you end up having to ride out all the bucks, but at least you are ready for the storm.

Zajlani had never bucked, reared, bit, or kicked (except soccer balls!) but after that, she bucked at unexpected times.

It was always after a nice ride, but with no stimulus I could ascertain. Very few horses had been able to get me off, but she dropped me any number of times.

With no warning or the apparent muscle-tensing windup that comes before a bucker's binge, she bucked in the funniest, effective, home-grown way that always caught me off guard. Coming in cheerful as always, with no apparent event to cause it in a ride, it mattered not the terrain or surroundings, but at some point, without dropping her neck and with no other warning, she'd instantly start spinning, simultaneously rocking sideways, back and forth, suddenly kick out, crow hop to the side, then she'd start bouncing around in very complete circles in the silliest mincing little steps, then leap up kicking out with all fours, land, and start sunfishing for reals, grunting and squealing like a pig.

If I survived the initial surprise, it was hell to stay on, not only because she didn't move the same way two jumps in a row, so you couldn't second guess what exactly was coming next, but whatever happened, the impromptu appearance of that little staccato horse *zapateado* flamenco she pumped out in a perfect butt-swinging circle, while wiggling her head and beeping and grumbling like an angry porcupine always made me laugh so hard I couldn't concentrate on staying mounted, which ended with my butt eating the dust.

I think a tick would've dropped off for the hilarity of such creative weirdness.

But even then, however she got you off, she never ran off to graze or disappeared running into the world like a lot of horses. She always came over to make sure I was alright and let me catch her just fine and then after adjusting the saddle, which would have slipped a bit, she'd take you home without a hitch and no more antics.

What a mystery it was; I couldn't quite figure it all out. I checked my saddles for splinters, stickers, cactus spines, burrs, bugs, loose tacks, and went over all my buckles, billets, and cinches searching for pinches, for any pokey things. I changed bridles, registered my boots, changed stirrups, changed bits, but nothing seemed to help and I couldn't find anything that might inspire this seemingly untriggered recent binge of ornate bucking.

Finally one night, my pelvis throbbing, I lay there thinking it all out. Probably nothing could be done about it, that's just the way she was.

But she didn't do it for any reason I could see and certainly not on cue and not every time we rode, but only on longer rides, but then not all of them. So what was there on some longer rides where she bucked, that was different from the other longer rides when she didn't? Was the saddle tree ill-fitting and rubbed her wrong? I checked it, but no. Even so, why not then every day?

Whatever it was, I didn't find out, surmising that the "many worded" reservation Barb mare, granddaughter of the great, wild, cliff-living Abalone stallion, just loved the delicious feeling of bucking, talking, grunting, and got a kick out of seeing her friend hit the ground, hurt, and laughing, just like horses do with one another.

Everyone else was asleep. The night was clear and it was late; the fragrant *sabina* wood loudly popping in the tipi fire. We slept in the tents in summer; I heard the horses snuffling, the boreal owl winnowing his snipe imitation, and Jupiter bright through the smoke flap hole helping to pull the beauty of a wider consideration into view, but then exhausted, I too slept.

Chapter 16

The Pocket Watch Mare

Around three thirty in the morning, in that magical
pool of non-sequential time, where half asleep, somewhere
between a dream and a brainstorm one's mind still suckles
from two mothers: one, the free rolling windy mind of the
wild earth who knows; and the other that ever-restless, clever,
tool-maker of our own distant past that still lives somewhere
in all our bones that's always trying to figure everything out,
I was eased awake into the crickets' thinning harangue from
a long dream of my father's father's Native mother ordering
me to "time" the route of a mule. A little more awake and full
of hot black tea, her voice still rang in my head—flushing a

forgotten detail out of the thicket of my recent memory, which in turn caused a theory to wriggle more clearly into view. A theory that sent me searching for my father's father's pocket watch to test that theory about the origins and possible remedy for Zajlani's mysterious buckery binge.

We had but one, very cheap, tinny, wind-up alarm clock that was used in dark winter mornings to ensure the kids got to the school bus on time, but it was too big and awkward to carry on a ride.

My father tried everything to get me to wear a watch. Having grown up in the so-called Great American Depression, where everything was once again more precious for its absence, my father prized a lot of things he felt were of the "basic" needs for any true adult survival. Though a tremendous admirer of every aspect of Nature, like others of his generation, he was convinced certain gizmos and small American inventions were somehow absolute necessities for human existence, never mind that we lived surrounded by Natives who did all their cooking on wood fire stoves and in adobe hornos, made most of their own clothing and shoes, still hunted a bit, and farmed—by hand and hoe—a lot of their food.

After a visit to my father's house, it was rare indeed if you didn't leave loaded up with flashlights (batteries in), several cans of evaporated milk, a sack of apples, a gallon of water, an electric shaver, and of course, if he saw you without one,... a wrist watch.

My father thought it an uncivilized abomination that I, who was clean-shaven, didn't use an electric shaver! The funny thing is that he always had a full beard and never shaved, but he always had a pile of reserve electric razors and made me take a new shaver every time I came, thinking I shaved with a safety razor because I didn't have the gizmo. The same applied to watches.

To my father's immense, Ohio raised American frustration it embarrassed him if someone, especially his oldest son, had to ask another person for the time. He thought I hated the time constraints of civilization so much, that in rebellion I wouldn't wear a watch. Like all the Natives that surrounded us, I wore silver jewelery instead. Some even wore silver and turquoise watch bands with a watch. Not I.

To humor him I gave them all a try, but watches I could never wear. Every watch my dad gave me ended up bashed to bits in our active life style or, if they survived, the old windups would just die within the week, the self-winding watches were more creative and would all start running backwards, and all the others had batteries that would swell up, leak, or explode, overloaded on whatever juice it was I emanated, so it wasn't just that I didn't use a watch; I actually couldn't wear a watch.

The life I led had so little need for big-city measured time anyway. There was, however, one personal time-piece I owned: my grandfather's over-sized, gold Elgin pocket watch with the gold chain. Besides his general nature, his love of horses, and his frustration with civilization's machine dependent, Native-killing ways, that watch was all that I'd inherited from that farming half-Moravian, half Lenape individualist. I prized that once ornate relic, all worn smooth, more because of his memory than its prodigious capacity to keep accurate, white-man time.

But, it was for that ability of this beautiful old watch that caused my predawn campaign to find it, for it was indeed strange that my deceased grandfather's hundred-year-old watch was the only watch that liked me and that would loyally count the hours, minutes, and seconds for me, just as it had for him, and all without a single hitch, when my father's modern watches would have nothing to do with me.

The question was, given how much I regarded that watch, in all the shuffle of life, I could not recollect in what special place I had laid that precious thing to keep it safe when my Father had handed it down to me a couple of years before.

The first purple light of dawn had barely begun to light the walls, so trying to keep my search unobtrusive, to let people sleep, I held my breath and pushed through the place, using my arm to look in a quiet sort of weasel like fashion. It wasn't in my wall bags, nor in the wooden chests, or in our cabin, not in the glove box of the truck, or in our hidden money box in the stone chamber in the ground.

The morning star was really bright and Orion was rising on the horizon; I stopped my search and prayed to all that beauty and then it dawned on me.

Right where I had hidden it when my Father passed it to me, there it lay, right among what we considered the most precious of all we had: nestled inside a little velvet sack, inside another sack at the very bottom of my handwoven sack of corn seeds from Guatemala, held inside yet another great bundle of all my long-stashed Holy things sat old Edward Prechtel's old pocket watch given him the day he left his life as a brakeman for the trains, to settle with my Irish grandmother, to sharecrop on a little farm of red wine grapes and vegetables. The diameter of half a Valencia orange, it was a big pocket watch with very legible numbers and a very ample knob, which made it very satisfying to wind. The only time I'd met my grandfather he let me wind it, which at the age of four I could hardly manage.

The sun was up, I slowly wound up the clock and slipped the heavy old lozenge into my pants pocket, clipped the substantial chain to my belt loop and headed into make breakfast for everyone, who'd been raised from their dreams by my quest.

Six weeks before, just one day before her bucking episodes commenced, the moment had arrived when I deemed Zajlani ready enough for riding. Because she was now rideable in a fairly manageable way, just to see how she would do, I thought to test her on a long ride to a small, old, cave spring whose sacred water I revered. But I had another motive as well: to break in a beautiful new saddle I had just finished building, along old time methods, to the measurements of her Ladyship's very own back.

These original *Mesta* horses were built in such a way, so subtle and distinct from all other horses, that no modern saddles could be found to fit them. Saddles for Arabians didn't fit, saddles for ponies didn't fit, three quarter bars on Quarter Horse saddles didn't fit, Thoroughbred saddles didn't fit, nothing fit because these old time Indian finessed *Mesta* horses were their own phenomena. In the 16th, 17th, 18th and the beginning of the 19th century they were the *only* horses in the American West, numbering in the millions, and saddles that fit them were everywhere. Now that only a handful of these real Cow Ponies existed, where had all those saddles gone?

It was not that these old time *Mesta* Indian crafted horses were *too small* or that their withers were too narrow or too low like a donkey or that their backs were too short. None of any of that was the case, as was claimed by the more recent type of saddle makers who couldn't quite see the situation as it was. Saddles are no longer made to fit a particular horse, like the old days. Types of standardized saddles for standardized *types* of horses are what they make these days. Since these types of Spanish/Indian horses had been intentionally extirpated from the American mind and written out of the landscape, their saddles were tossed into junk heaps or hung up in museums as relics of by-gone-days. For me those days were not gone, some of those horses were still here, and so was I. But their saddles were nowhere to be found!

What did matter was that the relationship of the particular angles of the logarithmic slope of the spring of the Indian pony's ribs to the slope of his withers, combined with the distinct pitch of the angle on the tight coupling of his back, was of such a very unique and interdependent geometry, that only by treating this uniqueness as a legitimate dimensionality for a legitimate *type* of horse, could a saddle in current times be made to function in a way that didn't compromise these little horse's tremendous agility and hurt their backs. Even later on when I talked saddle makers into measuring my Barbs for a saddle, the saddle makers would stare in disbelief and declare with immense disgust that such dimensions were unnatural and refuse to make saddles that conformed to those specifications. A lot of this was simple, racist hatred of Indian/Spanish horses by a certain cadre of whites, which was even wired into their equipment. These saddle-makers would only make saddles to fit the big, wide-chested horses that were ridden by those people, who on those horses, killed off all the Indian horses and their owners. But it was also just a smoke screen to cover up a general unwillingness to admit that this older type of horse had to be ridden in a very different balance and fashion, with a particular skill they didn't have or think they should want.

But be that as it may, I still needed a saddle that fit Zajlani, so... after months of jury rigging modern saddles with inadequate extra padding and failing to find anywhere a saddle to fit this little mare, I racked my brains trying to remember: "what were those saddles we had that had fit these little powerful horses in my youth?" They'd all been discarded because, of course, those saddles fit none of the horses the people were now riding: "east coast" horses, so to speak.

Everywhere I went I kept my eyes open for any old, forgotten, unwanted saddle dangling from a ranch fence, adorning a stall; saddles as left-over relics in families who could still remember the days when these little horses were the only horses in the giant neighborhood of the American west. For the most part they were all pretty beat-up and warped, but I bought their skeletons very cheap to study them. Eventually I found three fairly solid, very old, worn out saddles with unbroken trees: the first was a beautifully made, but badly trashed Northern Mexican saddle from the 1830's; another was a still viable New Mexico duckbill saddle tree from the 1840's; and a post Civil-War era original Eddelman roping saddle from Texas.

None of these old wrecks were really saddles, because all the rigging was gone and what remained of any hide covering was ruined and crisped like bacon by time's sure cooker. I tore off all the old leather rigging, skirting, and rawhide and by following the same general patterns and methods of fastening of what I had pulled away and re-using the same hand-forged rigging rings, I was able to refit all three of these frames into brand new saddles, with new rawhide on the trees, covered in new, vegetable-tanned leather. After adding some hand-hammered silver and homemade box stirrups big enough to accommodate my big winter boots, they were an elegant sight. Both traditional and yet still something of my own invention.

To my great delight and the physical relief of horses built like Zajlani, all three saddles fit her and all her relatives like a buckskin glove. For the first time in half a century—no matter what height or age of horse—these saddles never bruised or slid or banged on the withers of an old *Mesta* descended horse. They fit so well that I never again used any other kind except the ones I myself built. Over time I was able to get saddle trees carved to match the coordinates of these antiques and I continued to turn them into even better saddles.

All new saddles squeak, but saddles built in the old, original fashion really squeal. In a constant chorus of whispering wheezes for every single motion of the horse that doesn't even let up when the horse is standing quietly; even their calm breathing squeaks as it pulls every piece of leather into place. But after a month or two of riding, one day it all pretty much subsides; the creaks and squeals diminish and without any warning you can all of a sudden hear the birds singing again as you and your horse pick your way down the mountain. A green horse will often buck in terror at such relentless racket strapped onto his back. Zajlani, on the other hand, as green as she was, loved all the shiny handmade silver and because she loved being special and therefore revered wearing new gear, she rode along joyfully, like a little kid in new tennis shoes, squeaking all the way there and all the way back.

Freshly made saddles—especially those using the old style methods, where everything is tied and fastened purely with rawhide and hand tanned skin, without steel mesh, rivets, nails, screws, glue, staples, and toothed metal fasteners—during the period of breaking in, require frequent readjusting on the horse until everything has stretched over time and has finally molded right to both the shape of horse and her rider and their given motion and style of riding.

That first, long ride of some six hours round trip, while wearing her noisy new saddle, we had no occasion when Zajlani went into her bucking routine.

After so many nights of trying to conjure every possible reason she could have for starting to buck, in one situation here and now and not there and then, I deduced that she seemed to buck only on long rides, after that first long one, or sometimes on certain short ones, but only coming home. Was it the new saddle? Did it pinch after a while as she heated up?

So today, with old Ed Prechtel's pocket watch in place, we'd go on that same route—to the same exquisite high desert cave, out of whose mouth bubbled clear, clear water, in whose roof were swallow nests, then full of baby swallows, now all flown—and we'd check to see what, if anything might have instigated that funny strawberry roan mare to buck. We would do everything exactly the same way, with exactly the same amount of rest, the same gaits, to the same stopping places.

So I mounted, and leaning to the side, pulled up the chain to lift out the old watch from my *lance-side* pocket, like a ships anchor, and checking the time, which was 8:30am, I popped the lid shut and pushed the old man's clock back into my jeans. We began to sail, climbing up and over the forested ridge behind our camp, onto the next ridge and down that ridge to the east, dropping steadily till we got to the sagebrush flats beneath and then lit out in a canter west for a couple of miles until we settled into a concerted, swift walk for two hours more.

The late summer was rich after September's rare, blessed rain. The gold of the chamisas and the purple of the asters, the thick crop of blue grama and the red haze of the love grass were the only differences from the springtime when we'd come before, but when we arrived, there at the base of the cliffs of large-grain sandstone, the charcoal spot where we'd boiled up our tea the time last was only barely visible for all the flowers. The little cave was impossible to discern from the base of the cliff, for it lay well hidden, but you could hear it's spring percolating and thudding up on the side opposite, its water falling into an underground ravine, disappearing again only four feet from where it bubbled out.

The clock said 11:30am, give or take a second. Amazing, exactly three hours from the camp.

Releasing both girths I pulled the noisy, good smelling saddle off, propped it end up on its swells and let the sheepskin and blanket to the ground. I loosely hobbled Zajlani's front legs and leaving a neck rope dragging twenty feet, removed her painted rawhide bridle and set her loose to a cheerful crunching as she grazed the shorter grasses—at the base of the rich drying grasses—of these open spaces between the mountains.

I got a tiny fire going, excavated my oversized tea boiling mug from the saddlebags, poured water in from my canteen, and set it to boil. I always steeped loose tea at home, but when riding distances it was easier and the tea tasted strangely better to me boiled and filtered through a scarf into my favorite horn cup that never broke in the saddle bags. I sat back to admire the land, drank tea, and filled my lungs on fall's mature breath in whose perfume winter's immanent arrival could be read as a certainty.

You could hear the desert fountain very quietly rumbling her song in the little cave overhead, while a mockingbird echoed far away in the steep basaltic ravine lining the Big River opposite our side of the cliff.

I scaled the sandstone wall on foot to see the Gods that live there within, small and looking back at me, their tiny eyes peering out of that magic hole and—after tendering my song and the offerings I'd brought with a prayer for the wellbeing of everything and for a good snowy winter—I turned to scan and breathe in the wide world beyond. Some fifteen antelopes grazed far off out in the valley, in front of whom, I could barely make out what I took to be a little band of wild donkeys in a dusty streak tearing straight toward us.

Like a scared squirrel, I scurried back down the cliff to get to Zajlani fast, hoping I could get there before the donkey herd overtook us, for the wild male burros are awfully fierce and impossible to beat off if one decides he wants your mare.

So I packed up, saddled, and bridled frantically, checked my watch, almost 1:00pm, mounted and started cantering homeward by a different route, but the same one we used on our first visit.

Though they couldn't have seen us from the side of the cliff they were trotting in on, they had no doubt smelled Zajlani and once they reached the spring above and saw me mounting, one foot in the stirrup, the mare already moving off to run down below, the band of donkeys crashed carelessly over the crest, down the slope, and chased us. Their heads straight up and bobbing, with ears back and teeth bared, screaming and honking for war, the entire band galloped after us in a concerted pursuit.

Burros can run a lot faster than you think and luckily Zajlani did think it, and yelling right back at them in top decibel range, she took us away at a full gallop, at a speed we'd never before achieved and when one of those long-eared demons got close enough, she leapt forward off the ground and mid-air in the terrible dust we were all raising succeeded in clipping the lead burro in the jaw with a wicked rear kick. This donkey collapsed and rolled, body blocking his kin, who finally turned and gave up the chase. Only wanting to push us out of their territory in the first place, all of them headed back to the spring to drink, still braying and giving us a piece of their mind. The kicked one getting back to his feet and shaking his head straight, headed back with the rest, pulling up the rear, his tail gyrating like a propeller.

But the herd's badass stallion donkey wasn't giving in and he just kept on running after us biting my little mare's butt and she kept kicking at him, still running. Zajlani had been holding out on me, for she was a horse of unexpected great fleetness indeed, and luckily enough, exceedingly agile and sure footed, for on this route sharp beds of lava rock rose up wickedly, laying right on the trail through which one normally took a long time to pick one's way. Full of boulders pitted with sharp glass bubbles and razor edges all around, they formed a labyrinth of obsidian glass, of which any one of the thousand stones could split a hoof open in a second or a person in half if you fell.

But yelling the whole way, Zajlani ran through them all just like a marine in a tire obstacle and kept running until we finally out-stripped the furious donkey stallion, who slowed, turned around, and fled back, bellowing all the way. For in his wisdom and macho paranoia he realized he was no longer in his own territory and knew we had now crossed over into some other donkey's country and that he stood to lose his own band of seven lady burros calmly resting back at the spring with their foals, to another herdless male cruising the area, while he foolishly chased some sexy, pheromonal, singing horse he could not catch. He disappeared away from us in little puffs of dust back the two miles we'd come from the spring.

Past the lava fields now, we were almost to the trees, still galloping, before we dared to slow down to an extended trot. I'd forgotten about the wild burro's in this area. The Department of Interior had exterminated one group of them, but there were still little bands of them around, often mixing right in with the small groups of wild horses, causing not a few, very tough, wild mules and jennys to appear. But like dust devils, they just appeared from nowhere, here now, then gone, then later right there in your night camp driving off your mares while you slept.

Before cars, trucks, and highways more people had Spanish burros to ride, pull carts and wagons, and do farm work than they had horses. They were so capable, cheap to buy, and easy to keep that everybody had a couple, but *nobody* kept an ungelded male donkey, because domesticated donkey stallions were even harsher than horse stallions to manage, never mind the wild ones. But even so, in the old days, people didn't need to keep stallions in order to get their lady donkey bred. They simply tied her in an open corral during her heat cycle and the "wind" would breed her, as they say. Because

the burros were so good at living in our big, open neighborhood of the American west, they went wild in a second when
mechanization and modernity took over people's minds.

When Zajlani and I started getting close to home, I pulled
up the golden, anchor-chain hitch to civilization's time piece
and realized, with all the hurrying high speed scurrying to escape the hooves and teeth of mad wild donkeys, that we were
a full twenty minutes too early to test my experiment! So, I
stopped and we made tea again. But this time underneath the
pines and firs and let our adrenalin settle a bit, after which
the world was so balmy, delicious smelling, and relaxing that
both of us ended up napping.

Zajlani woke us both with a snort and when I checked the
time, we would be five minutes over three hours by the time
we made it home.

During our halt I'd left the saddle on this time, intending
just to take a breather, so after packing up all our tea things,
(I say we because all my horses liked to drink a little tea as
well) I mounted up and we walked leisurely to our camp and
just as I suspected, exactly three hours from my last frantic
saddling up at the spring and only a quarter of a mile from
home, Zajlani tried to spin, then dance and buck, but this time
I was waiting for it and countered her every motion. Congratulating my Lenape ancestress on her brilliance in my dream,
I dismounted, completely unsaddled, counted to sixty then
resaddled, remounted, and walked home, calm and smiling,
Zajlani whinnying, saddle squeaking. It was a beautiful day,
the gorgeous yellow and purple of a New Mexico fall, the

bubbling Gods of holy springs, antelopes, chased by screaming vicious donkeys, galloping and dancing through lava bed
cavaletti, good tea, a short nap and at least one mystery of
Zajlani's mind finally revealed.

It all made perfect sense now: at least in a more Indian
horse kind of intellectual way. What I had here, by the name
of Zajlani, the mockingbird horse, the many-worded horse,
was none other than a three-hour mare!

Horses are very nice to let any of us ride them, for it's not
written in nature that they should be ridden at all, much less
by a bunch of scared, complicated human monkeys. Or that
they are naturally built to serve us in the least, for its all an
unnatural imposition we put on them, for us to somehow gain
the liberty that we deprive them of in the process of getting
ours. It's a privilege to be allowed to ride, not a God given
right and we must bow our heads to the Goddess of Horses
and accept the deal she gives us.

Well, a new untouched horse of the old *Mesta* Indian landraced type learns so fast, that her would-be rider needs to be
just as quick of mind to correspond or we get into trouble really fast. Every flick of the wrists, every new sound, every new
smell, all your body motions, everything they see or do on the
very first day stays written forever in their big old memories.

Zajlani had never been halter trained or ridden, so everything we did for the first time had to be done the second time
the same way or somehow supplanted in her mind with a third
thing of equal value, that allowed her head to consider that the
initial sequence of ritual had been kept. Mares in particular

hold sequence as very important and if a dull teacher over-looks this ritual need, a horse can get into a bad rut real fast. Whereas with an astute teacher from the beginning, this need for dependable sequence in a natural horse can make a real good riding horse. It all depends on if an awake horse has people of equivalent brilliance for companions. Humans of all types and walks of life can be very brilliant, but because the comfort of modern life has dulled our capacity to perceive natural subtleties, most human brilliance is lost or only used for personal gain.

I'd been riding this little girl mare mindful of her heat cycles and since at that time I owned no stallions this was less of an issue. But if the first time I saddled her she'd been in heat and I had succeeded in getting on and riding, we stood a big chance of having to wait twenty days until her heat cycle returned to saddle because by her natural mind, saddling only went together with her being in heat. Out of heat she would have fought the saddle because it hadn't been done that way at first. One has to think these things out. They pile up into vast layers of entangled complications if we don't.

This was not the situation with Zajlani because I'd always watched for things like that. But in the middle of her learning how to ride, I did change saddles at the onset of her very first long ride. With that new, squeaky saddle we rode together three hours to the cave and spring, and then unsaddled.

She loved the feeling of that new saddle on her back, which conversed with her out loud as much as she with it and in her sequence-ordered logic knew that with this saddle came the rules that it had to be removed every three hours because in her training it had happened that way the first time I'd strapped it on. To have that good saddle on her back again, she must be re-saddled every three hours or something was amiss, it would not be the same experience or saddle. If this order had been destroyed and she had not been unsaddled when the three hours were up, the treaty would have been broken, she would pull out all the stops and buck and flap like line-dried laundry in a tornado!

So all I had to do was make sure I took the saddle and blankets completely off, then resaddle her every three hours with that same saddle and never again did I endure another buck out of her! If I used a different saddle, the rules all changed because the different saddle wouldn't fit and though she didn't like it, she would just plod along and could not make up any speed because it hurt her back so much to do it, but she never bucked. Whereas the great saddle I'd made just for her and her relatives fit her perfectly and so she could freely move faster and more agilely with me up on her back because I also made the saddle with my own riding posture on this horse in mind, so I had a better seat as well. But that good saddle required that it be removed and re-saddled every three hours or she would get worried and get you off if she could. The only trouble with all of that, though it was all wonderfully practical in a way, was that she did not accept the saddle being changed at an earlier time, it had to be pretty damned close to three hours or it wouldn't count! You could actually set your watch by it if you had one.

The beautiful, strawberry roan, *Mesta* Indian mare called Zajlani, Many Words, the Mockingbird became better known around our place as the Three Hour Mare. She was the first horse of the same amazing old-time kind we'd been riding on the Rez as kids that I had ever personally owned.

She became a very good friend to me for several years, but eventually when my life got more spread out, she was stolen from me. Years later she resurfaced on the Piegan Reservation with new Native owners outside Browning, Montana who had innocently received her from the thief.

I found out years later when I saw her photo in a coffee table book, being kissed on the nose by a Blackfoot gentleman. He looked like he loved her a lot, so after all that time I didn't pursue getting her back; I just let it all go. But she looked like she was wondering where her saddle went, and so did I, because that wonderful saddle was stolen by the same people who stole her.

While Zajlani was a great one—and like in the olden days where good horses, since they are made of motion, always got around, either by raid, trade, or misadventure—she, in the end, was the sister of Blue Medicine, who when he finally came to me, would stay on till his last day.

...And here begins
The Wild Rose: Stories of My Horses, Volume II.

Glossary

Arriéro (Spanish; pronounced Ah-ree-err-o) – a drover. Person who manages a string of pack or baggage animals: mules, burros, horses, etc. A well established career throughout the Spanish speaking areas of the world, especially traversing mountainous areas where no wheeled traffic could pass. Like sailors they have been famous for their songs, poems, stories, and their knowledge of the stars.

Barb Horse – at present day a confusing term for more than one kind of horse whose meaning has been clouded by various European horse registries claiming Barb ancestries for horses that actually originated from Central Asian Nomadic stock, which are not *Barbs*. Technically a Barb Horse referred to horses historically belonging to any of the many diverse Berber peoples, both nomadic and settled, both inland and along the *Barbary coast* of Morocco, Algeria, Libya, parts of Egypt, etc.

The famous Spanish horse of the Middle Ages and Renaissance no longer truly exists in Spain due to devastating horse epidemics during the Napoleonic Wars and the 19th century Spanish Civil War, but was originally a fine Barb type horse. The original *Mesta* horses of the Americas, the Cow Pony of the American Southwest, was often called a Barb by the cattlemen who very intelligently recognized these powerful, small, beautiful horses for what they were, a North African Spanish horse of mostly Barb descendancy that came

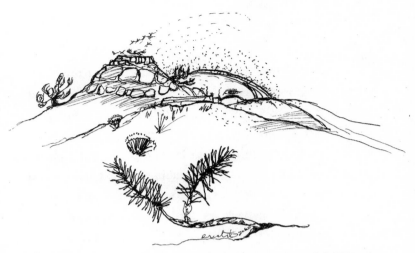

to the Americas before they largely disappeared in Europe during the terrible horse epidemics.

Bramadero – Spanish from the word *brama* meaning the fertile period or sexual heat in a female animal. A bramadero is a very sturdily built breeding pen with a stout post buried in the middle where a bull and heifers are brought together for mating. But in the Spanish speaking Americas, a bramadero more often refers to the post or *brake* where horses begin their training. See *breaking a horse*.

Breaking a horse – bad pulp fiction about horses has confused the notion of what breaking a horse actually means in English. A horse that is broken is not *broken* like a twig, but tamed to be ridden. While there are horses that have most certainly been wrecked, destroyed, their souls reduced to sulky bitterness and this is all atrocious and uncalled for, none of this has anything to do with what people mean with the term *breaking a horse*.

Breaking a horse arises from an historical semantic mix-up and orthographic inconsistency. Originally the word *breaking* as in breaking a horse was written *braking a horse*, referred to *softening* or *suppling* something, as when softening an untanned hide to turn it into leather. *Braking a hide* was part of the old European leather tanning process and was carried out by two individuals who, from opposite sides, pulled a previously *cured* skin back and forth over the top of a smooth stake to soften it. Looking like a five foot high gigantic polished baseball bat set deeply into the ground, this stake was known as a *brake* in German, Celtic, and eventually English. When hide tanners went about softening a skin, toward the end of the tanning process, they called it *braking a skin* not *breaking a skin* i.e., softening a hide on a brake. Training a *raw, green* horse properly, stage by stage, over a period of time to slowly make a suppled, tame riding horse was likened to the many stages of courting a raw freshly removed skin of a large animal called a *green hide* to slowly turn it into a beautiful, pliable, strong, good smelling, and very useful piece of leather. The last stage of hide softening and horse gentling was also called the gradual *braking* or suppling of the horse, like a calf skin, into a pliable and useful riding horse!

While a *horse braker* was originally a person who could *gentle* a horse, a horse *breaker* on the other hand was a term invented by pulp fiction writers to designate those people who used rough methods to *dominate* strings of green horses for quick sale by bucking them out till they couldn't move and selling them as *broke*.

A horse tamer was a person who *bucked* horses out. A horse gentler was a person who softened horses and accustomed them to the saddle or harness. It's good to know your own history. But in the American West a *broke* horse still means a horse that's been gentled, softened, and made pliable to ride, not a horse ruined and dominated into submission.

Bozal (Spanish; pronounced bow-sáhl) – horse riding equipment. In the Americas, a braided leather or rawhide noseband set in a headstall. Shaped like the frame of a Native snowshoe, the *bozal* is used instead of a bit to train a horse to respond to being steered with reins by pressure on the nose without the danger of ruining a horse's mouth. Usually, once the horse rides well on the *bozal*, a bit is added and a very thin *bozal* replaces the original noseband. The theory is that the horse learns to respond to very subtle rein cues without having to be cued by any direct pressure on the bit.

Cabestro (Spanish) – means different things in different parts of the world. But generally it refers to a some type of horse halter, a rig that fits over a horse or donkey's head, running from behind the ears to a noseband and fastens under the jaw. In some places, *cabestro* refers to a headstall. See halter.

Chicken snare saddle – in the old American West the word *chicken* in settler English and the corresponding *gallina* in post-colonial Spanish, did not always refer to a domesticated chicken but more often than not to some species of grouse or prairie chicken. Thus, even on a map today, the Gallina Mountains, Gallina River, or Gallina Canyon, Chicken Creek, etc. all refer to the wild galliformes, not leghorns or barred rocks. The early Spanish and the first Anglo-Americans in the west learned to trap and eat these wild ground birds from the original Native peoples of the area they invaded. One type of these traps had two bars connected by two bent branches and a net stretched over the whole that would snap shut like a clam when tripped by a bird trying to eat the corn with which it was baited.

Thus the *quick to make* rawhide covered antler and wood-slab saddle made by many tribes for riding or packing was likened to a prairie chicken snare. Thus the name chicken snare saddle. Very useful, actually difficult to craft, and with a good furry sheepskin or pelt, not too bad on the bottom. Native American women's saddles were for the most part exquisite works of art and, although made of elk antler as well, they were very tall and a different thing altogether.

Coloratura (Italian, Spanish, English) – opera singing term for the improvisational trills and ululations at the ends of phrases in old Italian operas.

Coursing – an unofficial term for a very official horse gait. People think that saying a horse is *coursing* over the land just means the horse is galloping fast, but *coursing* is a particular way to cover land. Some people think horses have only four gaits: walk, trot, canter and gallop. But horses around the world have all sorts of gaits associated with types and breeds. There is the tölt, paso fino, amble, marchalarga, walk-run, the rack, not to mention unfortunate, synthetically enforced gaits, to name just a few.

While individual foals are often born with extra gaits unknown to the parents, for the most part in my neighborhood, our horses move in the following gaits:

A walk, which has a two beat rhythm.

A trot, which has a single alternating staccato beat.

An Indian Shuffle, which is a cross between a trot and a rack that is a smooth motion through sand that rocks from side to side.

A lope is a slow canter in three beats, lovely and fast enough.

A full canter, a fast three beat motion, the best gait of all.

A gallop, a fast four beat divided into two.

A run, a smooth very fast, reaching gait.

A *course*, just like a jackrabbit or leopard runs, by reaching forward past the ears with the hind legs and pushing powerfully forward while reaching way forward with both front legs and powerfully pulling forward. Once well established its just like a fast moving river and feels pretty much like flying because the horse is in the air three times longer than his feet are on the ground. So coursing across the land, a herd of wild horses can look like a flash flood of flesh, fur, and dust. Very majestic to ride and see.

Crop (English) – a thin, semi-flexible, short whip used to cue a saddle horse. A constant presence and fetish of status in northern European horse riding. Originally made of a thin piece of dried bull penis covered in braided black silk, but later made from whale baleen and braided silk, nowadays most are fiberglass and polyester. Any European derived saddle riding tradition is always done with a crop, often a symbol of gentry, imperial domination, and European cavalry. While all horse cultures have some sort of riding whip to urge their horses, more often they are beautifully adorned, more whip-like, and works of art in themselves. Worn more as a piece of tribal jewelery than a functional tool, compared to these an English crop is a rather anal, puritan-looking, sneering twig.

Delicia (Spanish, Southwestern "English") – the lusciousness of something, the deliciousness.

Diné (Diné) – a Diné word for themselves. Also known as Navajo. The actual meaning of the word Diné in Diné language is complex. It is now politically proper to designate any Navajo person as pertaining to the Diné tribe. But the word Diné doesn't actually imply Navajos, or humans. It refers to the living form of anything. For instance, Lightning Diné, or Fir Tree Diné, or Corn Beetle Diné, or Rain Diné. Different tribes are *Paiute* Diné or *Taos* Diné, *Mexican* Diné etc. To distinguish themselves, the Diné of today generally say *Ta'á Diné* to signify their particular *Navajo* Diné.

Dinétah – old Diné word for their tribal homeland. A euphemism sometimes used by non-Navajos for the landscape where one *belongs*.

Dorsal stripe (English) – a type of horse marking, used to signify the dark narrow line (red, black, grey) that some horses exhibit that runs from the mane down and over their withers, right on top of their spine, to the tail. Considered by veterinary science to be a primitive horse coat pattern from before the Pleistocene era.

Ergot (Latin/English) – the strange English language term for the little bony protuberances at the rear of the fetlock on a horse's foot, which along with the "chestnuts" found on the insides of the horse's forearms constitute what remains of the original three other toes of the prehistoric ancestors of our now single-toed horses.

For a lot of tribal horse people worldwide, these ergots and chestnuts are considered to be very powerfully charged with medicine.

Gallo and **Gallo Horse** (Spanish) – The word *gallo* (pronounced gah-yo), means literally a rooster in Spanish. But a *gallo* is also the colloquial name for an ancient game played on horseback that has far-flung origins among horse people throughout North Africa, Europe, Central and North Asia.

When the Spanish colonial culture came to what later was called the American Southwest they brought with them a lot of their animals, cultivars, tools, and methods for taking care of all that, their religion and a lot of customs. Not all of these things flourished in their new setting, but some things stuck and became so much a part of Native cultures and Hispanic post-colonial life that people sometimes forget their origins.

Horses, long-horned cows, churro sheep, Angora goats, big red hogs, rabbit hounds, steel knives, axes, hoes, pulleys, shovels, pliers, scissors, nails, wheat, barley, grapes, peaches, plums, cherries, radishes, haba beans, parsnips, carrots, oats, peas, floor looms, spinning wheels, playing cards, chess, to name just a few all combined with the amazing plants and minerals, tools and methods of other people the Spanish had overrun farther south, when all of these things merged in turn with the equally rich and capable cultures already in place in what is now New Mexico, the resulting culture became the unique phenomena it is today.

One of the things that really took off was the raising of chickens. With chickens, one doesn't only end up with eggs and delicious chicken recipes, but roosters. You only need a single rooster to breed forty to fifty hens, but with a lot of broody hens you end up with a lot of roosters. Just like horses, unless you castrate them, you end up having to deal with a lot of fighting males. Like stallions, roosters are very fierce and jealous of their females. A castrated rooster, called a capon, is an eating speciality of certain peoples, especially the French and Italians and formerly the English. They grow real big and taste very good.

But in our area the yearly over-population of roosters was annually dealt with by their part in an ancient horse game, brought by the Spanish, which was then further finessed into Pueblo spiritualism. In our area of New Mexico, on the Saint's day of San Antonio on June 14, San Juan on June 24 and Santiago on July 24, great contests and exhibitions of horse riding expertise were carried out, called the *gallo*: the rooster.

In this game, after villagers donate a great number of live roosters, up to three hundred Native riders and their little horses line up to have a chance to pull a live rooster out of a hill of sand where he has been buried up to his neck. Riders canter past the rooster, just to the left, then without stopping and leaning way over to the right, attempt to pull the entire flapping bird out of the ground as they pass. Most fail to grab the wily dodging head of the rooster, but when one is successful, this rider then grabs the bird tight so as to avoid the rooster's wicked spurs and in the same moment with a knotted cloth for a quirt, the rider starts his horse galloping as fast as he can and in any design of motion to avoid the thundering mass of the rest of three hundred riders chasing him and his horse and the flapping rooster who are all dedicated to rudely wresting the rooster away from him by whatever means possible. At break-neck speeds the riders dodge and hit, ride sideways, and do all sorts of maneuvers, the rooster often serving as a club to beat off assailants.

The flapping of the rooster only served to make all the horses go faster.

The goal, if you got a rooster out of the ground and got away, or succeeded in taking it away from some other rider in the thick dust and swirling milieu of horses, was to ride like hell to the house of the girl you loved the most and throw the rooster in through her adobe doorway, at which point the rooster was already dead, or killed by the lady of the house and all pursuit was called off and the next round of riders went after the next rooster in the very long line of buried roosters. The *gallo* could go on in this way for even eight to ten hours making it also a test of tremendous endurance for both man and beast. The roosters thus distributed were plucked and stewed and taken by the sweetheart to the parents of the young man who had tossed the bird into her house as a kind of courting gesture.

In this game a lot of expert riding techniques were used, but riders often toppled from their horses, losing their seat while trying to retrieve a rooster. Newly proficient young riders, the heroes of the game, were always emerging to take the day, but a lot of big, rowdy middle-aged Indians, veterans of many *gallos*, were the admitted masters. Church bells were rung and bugles blown every time someone was fleeing with a rooster. And after a while all the previous winners had to ride single-file between two long poles, each maneuvered by two men on the ground. Between the tops of these poles a rope was stretched in whose center a live rooster was fastened. The idea was to stand up on your horse as you rode underneath this rooster that was held between the poles as he dropped and rose, grab the bird, jump back down into your saddle and once again run like hell to avoid a hundred riders on your tail trying to get the bird away from you.

To ride in the *gallo* you needed a really good horse and the short little *Mesta* Barbs were made for it. Like polo ponies, they had to be able to stand, but then respond in a flash, turn on a dime, move sideways and feint, stop and jump out, charge undaunted into other horses and into a huge crush of animals, then light out, like a hawk with a chicken, in a second without biting or striking, and never tire. It was extremely rugged, very exciting, and very heroic. There were a lot of broken noses, dislocated fingers, broken ribs. Sometimes riders were maimed in the fray and every few years someone was killed, usually dragged, caught in the stirrup, and smashed into a wall. But everyone riding in a *gallo* came out a little beat up and bloody, but smiling and excited. The horses loved the *gallo* with all the herd-like free-for-alls.

But a good *gallo* horse was always a prize animal. Funnily enough, when American-style rodeos began to dominate the *Western* scene, they were all called *gallos* by the locals, not rodeos. In some Native languages, such as Diné, a rodeo is still called *hoohai*: chicken. When I was a little kid it took me a long while to figure out why Navajos always called their much beloved rodeos the *hoohai* or chicken. "Hey, let's go rope at the chicken Martín!" It makes sense once you think about it, for at least where I grew up, in a full-on *gallo* there was a lot more wild horsemanship involved than any rodeo or horse event. Anyone who's seen or ridden in one can attest to the accuracy of that statement!

Of course when it comes to the Native ritual aspect of the *gallo*, there's a lot more to tell than the Spanish bugles, the bell-ringing, painting of the horses, the communal gift giving, the feasting, the anger contest, and a thousand more beautiful components, but in my experience all the charm and excitement that a large *gallo* inspires in New Mexicans and Natives seems to be lost on most modern, urban people, so I'll just leave it at that. You get the general idea. Anglos call the *gallo* a rooster pull.

Gelding (English) – a castrated stallion. Supposedly devoid of the testosterone driven fierceness of stallions and the unpredictable craze of mares in heat every 21 days, geldings are the world's most common form of riding horse. Most cultures geld male horses, keeping only a few intact stallions to further the line.

Granny gear (American slang) – compound low gear in old time trucks. Those vehicles had four forward gears and reverse. But first gear was so low and powerful, most people started their trucks in second gear, using first gear (granny gear) only for slow, very difficult terrain. Before four-wheel drive was common, granny gear was all we had.

Green horse – an untrained horse. See breaking a horse.

Grulla (pronounced grew-yah) – horse color from the Spanish word grulla or crane, as in sandhill crane. Typically a kind of holographic coat that reflects red or blueish overtones with dark legs, dark dorsal stripes, dark tail, muzzle, and mane. Crane colored.

Halter – a horse's headgear made of rope, leather, or webbing. Goes over a horse's head, behind the ears, buckling at the throat, used with a tie-on or clip-on lead rope to guide a horse to where you want and for tying up to hold a horse still while saddling. Not made for riding, just for moving a horse on the ground, though there are people who ride with halters and reins these days.

Hashmarks (Western American cowboy slang) – horse color term for any number of dark, parallel stripes that sometimes adorn the fur of a horse's forearm, like the chevrons on the shoulders and cuffs of military uniforms that signify rank. Along with *dorsal stripes*, *spider webbing*, and *smokey withers* or *cross*, *hashmarks* are thought to be throwback markings from prehistoric equines.

Headstall (English) – the leather head gear that holds a bit in a horse's mouth or noseband in place. Used for riding with reins attached to bits or noseband.

Horno (Spanish; pronounced O´r-no) – a wood fired outside oven. In northern New Mexico, horno signifies a large beehive shaped oven made of tufa or adobes plastered with mud; used to bake bread, *biscochitos*, cookies, prune and peach pies, to roast meat, squash, and sweetcorn. Everyone loves to eat what comes out of the horno.

In hand (English) – a common Euro-American riding term that signifies that a horse ridden or horses driven are responding to the signals of the rider or their driver by means of the reins held in the rider's or driver's hands i.e. the rider is in control.

The common spoken English expression denoting a situation that is out of control: things "have gotten *out of hand*," originally meant that a rider's horse was not listening and responding to the hand held reins and the horse was therefore *out of hand*, going berserk, ready to bolt, out of control.

Thus things are *in hand* or *out of hand*.

Lance-side – an old English horseman's term for what in all of Europe in their own languages is the original designation of what today is called the offside on a horse: the right side.

Because Medieval European knights and earlier North African and Arab knights kept their swords belted to the left to be drawn with their right hand and their lance butts socketed on the right side in a sheath-like holder strapped onto the front cinch or stirrup strap, they always mounted from the left holding onto the lance to get into the saddle.

While warrior cultures worldwide taught their children, boys and girls, to mount and dismount from either side (a very good policy), European descended riding traditions mount only from the left, this being "the on-side" and the right being "the offside", all motions militarily derived.

Mecate (Mexican Spanish; pronounced mek-ah-tei) – from the Nahuat *mecatl*, originally an Indigenous Mexican term for rope or cordage, usually expertly twisted from the fibers of the blades of certain species of maguey or lechuguilla plants. But, as a word, it gradually gestated to mean a three or two-ply rope, one inch thick, made of the mane hair of horses and about twenty foot long. When used in conjunction with the *jaquima* and *bozal*, it binds the whole headrig in such a way as to provide both a set of reins and a lead rope, all in one. American cowboys call it a McCardy.

But the word *mecate* used casually usually signifies a twenty foot rope used to halter horses *old style*, without a halter, by a couple of configurations to tie up a horse while saddling and bridling. Generally, a loop remains around the horse's neck and the slack tied up to the saddle while riding. This slack can then be let out while resting a horse or tied to a tree while the horse grazes and the rider boils up some tea or coffee. Just like tying up a boat. I grew up with the *mecate* and not halters.

Mesta (Spanish) – originally a co-operative of Spanish stock raisers who graze their animals in common and take turns watching over them and come together to co-operatively round up, move the animals, doctor them, and train them in the case of oxen or horses.

A kind of ancient Iberian grange where members met and voted on leaders and what to do with animals and who communally shared expenses. Because the livestock was generally herded in wild open areas and not held in fenced paddocks or pastures, some herders had to always be on the job.

Any animal raised in this style of open, wild grazing was

called in Spanish *Mesteño*. The word *Mesteño* eventually gestated into the American English word mustang. But originally a *Mesteño* horse was never an unprovenanced, ownerless, feral animal, but a horse raised in a *Mesta* herd watched over by *Mesta* rangers. Colonial Spanish horse raisers spread the institution of the *Mesta* to their colonies and Native populations continued raising their cattle and horses in this same time-honored way after Spain no longer claimed the area. We still did so in my youth.

It is interesting to note that the word mustang, even in standard American English dictionaries up until WWII signified a "small narrow-chested Spanish horse of great endurance and steady temperament from the American Southwest": basically identical to what a horse of the *Mesta* had always meant.

But Mustangs as *Mesta* horses disappear from the American consciousness after the 1940's and ever since any large clump of unowned, feral, American ranch horses, draught horses, and ponies running on public land have been called mustangs. Though some of these are interesting, they are not the same animal in the least.

Mare – mature female horse.

Oregano de la Sierra – a variety of Monarda, a mountain mint treasured by Northern New Mexicans for medicine.

Platica (pláh-tee-cah) Spanish for conversation. In New Mexico and other parts of the Americas platica can mean the distilled central meaning of what someone is trying to get across.

Proud flesh – when a horse experiences a gash, like cats, their bodies quickly self-bandage themselves and try to cover the exposed flesh by naturally producing a kind of thick gooey, very frothy, white substance that seems to keep out flies and dirt, but sometimes solidifies and cracks. Though it's part of the natural healing process, we generally wash it off to keep the wound filling with real tissue, which if given a chance horses admirably do.

Quirt (Southwestern American English) – cowboy foreshortening of the Spanish word *cuarta* signifying a short riding whip that can take any number of forms. The classic Mexican quirt has a wristband that attaches to a semi-stiff, tapered, braided shank about ten to fifteen inches long that has two, twelve to eighteen inch, latigo lashes attached at the bottom. Usually very ornately braided leather over rawhide, but sometimes five multi-colored strands of rawhide braided over a rawhide core, or even different colors of sorted horsehair braided over a braided rawhide shank, quirts can be quite beautiful. Different Native American tribes in North America made extraordinary customized quirts from pieces of moose antler and skin, elk antler, wood covered in brass tacks, buffalo or mountain sheep horn, all with lashes of stiff, brain-tanned neck leather or braided lashes and fancy beaded wristbands.

All over South America, particularly the Gauchos in Argentina, some Spaniards, various North African peoples, Turkmen nomads, Bashkir and Kyrgiz still make beautiful quirts covered in silver. Except for Gauchos, Chileanos, and American cowboys who ride with quirts and spurs, most quirt riding traditions don't use spurs to cue or motivate their horses, preferring the quirt to direct signals. The author is a quirt rider and quirt collector.

Rateros (Spanish American slang) – means thieves or pick-pockets. From the word for rat.

Roan (Anglified medieval Spanish word) – signifies a horse who is covered in two or more distinct colors of hair in tight formation so as to appear as a single color from a distance, but changes in tonality at different angles of the sun. There are red roans (white and red mixed), yellow roans (yellow and white), blue roans (reflective gray black and white), and grulla (black and red and white tightly mixed). A lot of color variations occur in roan patterns, some horses sporting five or six different coat color moltings of roan annually. There are many local terms for these like: coyote roan, strawberry roan, buttermilk roan, etc. The research is not all in on the real dynamics of roan coloration because in my own experience a totally different follicle function happens in the old *Mesta* roans that has seemed to defy veterinary science to date.

Sabina (Spanish) – the one seed juniper tree whose very fragrant, durable presence covers most of the area of Northern

New Mexico from 5,000 ft to 7,000 ft. Most people from tall tree or forested parts of the world have no respect for our little New Mexico *sabina* tree, but it forms a belt running the entire circumference of the Earth's land masses all the way from Manchuria and Mongolia through parts of Northern Europe into a lot of North America. Where it grows, it is universally considered very powerful good luck and health. The word *sabina* is also a modern horse color phrase.

Side saddle – this is a pretty strange rig invented for European ladies in that period when dress styles interfered with straddling a horse and when a woman straddling a horse was considered too *barbarian* and unladylike. All nomadic tribes had incredible woman horse riders, none of whom were stuck riding side saddles. You have to see a side saddle in action to understand it's function. But in short, it involves a rather bulky asymmetrical saddle with only one stirrup on the left, upon which a lady mounts by plopping her bottom into a tall side-facing cantle, after which she wraps her right leg around a kind of cushioned post protruding at about 10 o'clock from the pommel, so that both legs are essentially hanging from the left side of the horse. Very hard on a horse's back and strange looking in motion, but I've seen women who can really ride in one. Running from the 12th century to the 20th, where along with the riding habit (a gentlewoman's riding *costume*), wasp-waisted, baleen-corseting, slave ownership and of course a crop, it's part of European gentry horse history.

Snaffle/snaffle bit (English) (*Filete* in Spanish) – a basic bit used worldwide, in which pressure from the reins is directly on the bars of the horse's mouth. Developed by Proto-Scythian, Indo-European pastoral nomads three to four thousand years back, it was often the only metal (bronze originally) part of all their horse's harness. Composed mostly of two cheek rings that are attached to the headstall and reins, the rings are connected by two loose-sliding, metal bars jointed in the middle that runs over the horse's tongue, connecting the two rings. Considered the most gentle type of bit by most.

Saddle tree (English), or *fuste* (Spanish) – as used in this book, the core frame of a Southwestern saddle upon which are mounted successive layers of vegetable tan leather, rigging straps, cinches, stirrup leathers, and stirrups. Different cultures do it different ways. The Spanish use a basket frame, the American Southwest a wood frame. The saddles as described herein fit a horse only as good as its tree fits. A bad fitting tree is a bad fitting saddle.

Shinny – an Algonquin term used by Anglos for all the field hockey type games among all the Native tribes of the Americas. There are hundreds of styles and varieties. In New Mexico Pueblo culture shinny is a ceremonial game played at only a certain time of year by two large teams, whose players each wield two curved sticks and a special stuffed hide ball. It's loud, rowdy, never ends, and a lot of fun. There are man-forms and lady-forms.

Smokey withers – a Southwestern cowboy term for a horse with a dark, smokey patch of fur covering both sides of the withers, also called a smokey cross.

Spiderwebbing – wild, dark, squiggly lines along the forearms or withers of a horse's coat color, left over from early Pleistocene wild horse color.

Stallion – a sexually intact male horse or donkey who is capable of breeding mares. They are by nature very contentious, powerfully built, and a handful. It's rare to see people riding stallions without incident, but there are those that can and do.

Taboon (Russian) – used to describe the central Asian and nomad custom of raising horses in large mare and foal herds with a single stallion in wide open, unfenced territory. In taboon style, only geldings are ridden and few stallions kept and all mares are free to make more babies and to be milked to make *kumiss* or fermented milk liquor.

Taa Diné – see Diné.

Victorio – the non-Indian name of a very heroic and amazing Warm Springs Apache leader in the late 19th century whose attempted friendship with whites in Southern New Mexico landed him and all his people simultaneously at war with both the US army and the Mexican army. The accounts of Victorio's multiple escapes from captivity on horseback are legendary throughout the Southwest. Killed in a rearguard, decoy-action between two armies with a couple of his brave partisans, a strategy that allowed the last remnants of his particular band to escape into a mountain of Northern Mexico where they vaporized from view but where everyone says they are living still suspended in a happy magical aboriginal dimension.

Acknowledgments

While this entire trilogy is my attempt to toast and acknowledge all the horses, one by one, whose companionship have always given me the life and vitality of the "wide open ride", it would be remiss not to remember all those people, places, and animals who made the series *Stories of My Horses* possible.

Firstly, of course, a great blessing and thanks to the mystic soul of the open land, the fabulous skies, varied terrain, plants, and animals of my native New Mexico—whose Native peoples, Spanish speaking peoples, and select Anglo ranchers and cowboys were the parent cultures that made me and the horses what we became—and where all the events revealed in the text took place.

Next, I would like to thank the spirits of all the horses themselves, both dead and still living, whose accounts appear in these three books. Without them there would have been nothing to tell.

But...

I would like to thank even more those horses both dead and alive, whose stories do not appear in these books and to apologize to those horses whose stories did for those descriptions of equally dramatic episodes of their lives that I chose to leave out.

For old wisdom insists that it is never a good idea to empty out your sack of life's hard-earned memories all the way. Because good powerful memories are special: like sourdough bread starter, where from every batch you have to keep back a fistful of dough to make the next down the line. In the same way, worthy memories retained re-start the next section of one's life, leavening the dull grind of the present into a life fully lived from where the sack of stories worth remembering is re-stocked! Always good to keep back just a pinch for the next round.

Next, I'd like to send a big, two person *abrazo* for Liz Dwyer and Curtis Weinrich of North Star Press for their courage, love of beautiful books, love of story, and unique willingness to bring forth the three volumes of the *Stories of My Horses* in such a friendly, professional way. The literary freedom that this willingness has afforded me, allowing me to write and publish books so dear to my life with my unique language use still intact and outside the assigned genre slots where all my previous books are forced to reside, is like letting my "herd of words" out for a good delicious gallop across the forgotten soul of the American West after years of being corralled and contained in the tiny neurotic pens of east coast urban categories.

Then for my typist Susannah Hall in the UK, in honor of the most well-done, patient typing of my hand-written manuscripts, I would like to send a ride in the Queen's carriage (without the Queen, unless of course she insists on coming along) filled to the roof with the best organic butter, with bars of gold, and crates of freshly baked crumpets, tea, and a samovar strapped on top, driven by Hugh and Kayode, to the best of times and a picnic on a revived English eel river to kiss the elvers with their poetry!

Like everything else I endorse, my books are written by hand, with a pen on real paper. But this handwriting of mine is extremely idiosyncratic and hard to decipher to say the least, so it takes a special talent to read my initial screed, then type it, as written, into a program, have me rewrite on a hard copy, scan it and return it to Britain to retype, adding all my amplifications, going back and forth in this way for as many as seven rounds, for every chapter, whilst the manuscript grows into a bigger and bigger, newer and different manifestation over the months, until Ms. Hall discovers that she's been actually typing four books that I'm working on simultaneously!

I know Ms. Hall has a magnifying glass and some other manual aids for deciphering my scrawl, but no doubt she's been blessed by some supernatural to magically pull it off.

In short,

Her typing has been indispensable.

The author as illustrator would like to thank and acknowledge the late Hoke Denetsosie. In the 1930's and 40's this Diné artist developed a black and white, crow-quill pen style of illustrating the most beautiful editions of what were intended as bilingual Navajo/English primers for Native school children to learn to write both Diné and English. The most unlikely publisher for these forgotten books was the Department of Education, in the Bureau of Indian Affairs, Department of

Interior, in short the US Government! In a momentary flash of intelligent vision and good-heartedness the government simultaneously put out similar bilingual language books in other Native languages throughout the country, illustrated by artists of the corresponding tribes.

Though Denetsosie's work later became associated with cartoonists and other less worthy endeavors, his illustrations for the *Na'nilkaadi Yazhi* (*Little Herder*) series was more than a brilliant achievement and has never been equaled in originality. Like everything else after WWII, the government numbed up, and anxious in the cold war lost the thread, and what began as an amazing hopeful trend was utterly forgotten. A lot of amazing artists of all types emerged from this trend but most melted away, swept back under the carpet of the craze of technological progress.

But to me the original solutions Hoke Denetsosie came up with on his own, without coaching, or tutoring to illustrate the land and his people of those times was not only so subtly ingenious, but always an inspiration to me, more so because his drawings correspond very well with some of the territory and the moods of the land in which *Stories of My Horses* takes place. He was great, lived to be a very old Native rancher, well loved by his people but largely overlooked as an artist. I had to say something, for as I drew I always thought about him.

And now I want to say thank you to my little family,

To my beautiful eight-year-old boy Gobi, who loves our Mesteños as much as I do, who writes stories and edits as much as I do. To my wondrous eleven-year-old star-nebula loving daughter Altai, who also writes and edits as much as I do. And to their incredibly inspired teacher and beautiful determined mother, my wife, Johanna Keller Prechtel who using our special secret recipe of charred plants, mare, foal, and stallion manure compost has succeeded in growing a six-foot high broccoli thicket in December when even coyotes freeze solid like statues! (Old time horses are good for lots of things besides riding!).

For their love for me and their patience with my barrage of humor and their tolerance of the overly fierce delivery of my vision regarding the need for a more substantial and beautiful culture that permeates my every word and action cannot be adequately rewarded with any words I could ever conjure.

And to you gentle reader, for your love of the *wild open ride* over the wild open land and your willingness to eschew modern cynicism and ride with me in words, in ways and into places, where hardly any go anymore these days. But if we're not spiritually lazy, things can always change for the better and often do.

All blessings.

About the Author and Illustrator

As an avid student of indigenous eloquence, innovative language and thought, Martín Prechtel is a writer, artist, and teacher who, through his work both written and spoken, hopes to promote the subtlety, irony, and premodern vitality hidden in any living language. A half-blood Native American with a Pueblo Indian upbringing, he left New Mexico to live in the village of Santiago Atitlán, Guatemala, eventually becoming a full member of the Tzutujil Mayan community there. For many years he served as a principal in that body of village leaders responsible for piloting the young people through the meanings of their ancient stories in the rituals of adult rites of passage.

Once again, residing in his beloved New Mexico, Prechtel teaches at his international school, Bolad's Kitchen. Through an immersion into the world's lost seeds and sacred farming, forgotten music, magical architecture, ancient textile making, metalsmithing, the making and using of tools, musical instruments and food and the deeper meanings of the origins of all these things in the older stories, in ancient texts and by teaching through the traditional use of riddles, Prechtel hopes to inspire people of every mind and way to regrow and revitalize real culture and to find their own sense of place in the sacredness of a newly found daily existence in love with the natural world. Prechtel lives with his family and their Native *Mesta* horses in Northern New Mexico.

Martín Prechtel's previous works include: *Secrets of the Talking Jaguar*; *Long Life, Honey in the Heart*; *The Disobedience of the Daughter of the Sun*; *Stealing Benefacio's Roses*; *The Unlikely Peace at Cuchumaquic*; and *The Smell of Rain on Dust: Grief and Praise*.

Cover Painting, *Mother of Horses Bringing Home the Infant Sun and Moon,* by Martín Prechtel.